EIR (ISSN 0273-6314) *is published weekly (50 issues), by EIR News Service, Inc., P.O. Box 17390, Washington, D.C. 20041-0390. (703) 777-9451*

European Headquarters: E.I.R. GmbH, Postfach Bahnstrasse 9a, D-65205, Wiesbaden, Germany
Tel: 49-611-73650
Homepage: http://www.eirna.com
e-mail: eirna@eirna.com
Director: Georg Neudecker

Montreal, Canada: 514-461-1557

Denmark: EIR - Danmark, Sankt Knuds Vej 11, basement left, DK-1903 Frederiksberg, Denmark. Tel.: +45 35 43 60 40, Fax: +45 35 43 87 57. e-mail: eirdk@hotmail.com.

Mexico City: EIR, Sor Juana Inés de la Cruz 242-2 Col. Agricultura C.P. 11360 Delegación M. Hidalgo, México D.F. Tel. (5525) 5318-2301 eirmexico@gmail.com

Canada Post Publication Sales Agreement #40683579

Postmaster: Send all address changes to *EIR*, P.O. Box 17390, Washington, D.C. 20041-0390.

Signed articles in *EIR* represent the views of the authors, and not necessarily those of the Editorial Board.

How Obama Has Destroyed This Country

The Strategic Importance of Alexander Hamilton's Manhattan

During his November 7, 2015 dialogue with residents of New York City, Lyndon LaRouche began the proceedings with the following opening remarks:

Now we've come to a period in which there are various elements of destruction of the United States. The most important point right now, in terms of the entire United States, lies within the province of Manhattan. Manhattan was the birthplace of the United States, led by especially Alexander Hamilton. And everything that has come to the United States has been a product of the continuation of the principles of Alexander Hamilton and his associates, and every one of us, like me, who has had his own role in the leadership of the United States, briefly but significantly. And what's happened, is we have been destroyed throughout the United States.

The fact of the matter is that if you want to save the United States, if you want to save our nation and what it stands for, you have to concentrate on the mission of Manhattan, the mission of Manhattan which is defined by Alexander Hamilton. It's still there today. There's a lot of clutter in Manhattan; there are all kinds of people there. But at the same time, there is a coincidence which is good, as contrasted with incidence, which is intrinsically evil. And intrinsically evil means,—guess what? It means speculation, it means financial organizing. So these things have to be cleared away.

We have to recreate the United States to its intention, and recognize that Alexander Hamilton, even to this day, provides a model of excellence for what this nation represents. And you can find the essence of the United States in the founding role of Alexander Hamilton in creating the United States, including Manhattan.

And we have to therefore realize that other parts of the United States may be valuable parts of the United States, but they lack an essential part of what lies in Manhattan.

That is, not all of Manhattan is good, as everybody in Manhattan knows. Some of the worst crooks in the world have been in Manhattan. But we know there is in Manhattan still, a legacy of Alexander Hamilton; and it's not just the tomb that he has down there in the southern part of the territory. It's what he represents, and what has inspired other people, as by Alexander Hamilton's model, up to the present time.

Therefore, if we're going to solve this problem, we have to recognize that many parts of the United States are deficient. That is, they are deficient as trying to play a role as leadership. And the fact is, we've often destroyed the foundation of the United States, which is typified by Alexander Hamilton more than anything else. And you start to disperse the elements of the United States into local states, or fractions of local states, cults, and so forth, and what happens is you lose the original intention of the foundation of the United States, which was a miraculous development for all mankind. And the role of Manhattan in terms of bringing foreigners into the United States, and making them citizens in the United States, and spreading that influence from inside the United States, from Manhattan,—that is the particular genius which lies as a potential within the United States still today.

And therefore we have to understand that, and take those indications as a value. You know, we've had wars; the United States has been involved in several wars. Some of these wars were imposed upon the United States. The Civil War was a creation of the South, but it was a creation of an alien element, which took over and took authority *over* the United States. We had the first four Presidents after George Washington, Presidents in the young United States, who were crooks. We had a few great geniuses, but we had a plethora of crooks of various kinds. We have people who understand the tradition which the United States has represented in its best respects, but these are exceptional people, and they exist only as exceptional people, and they exist only by the contributing influence of these special people.

So we have to say, "This nation is *one* nation. It is not a division or separation of states within one nation. It is *one* nation." And that concept of one nation, which Alexander Hamilton typifies, with all the things that have happened otherwise in the history of the United States, all reduces to that one point. And Manhattan today contains a germ within Manhattan,—not the plethora of people in Manhattan, but a germ among that plethora within Manhattan,—typified by its exceptional persons: the people in the organization of Manhattan who represent something special in terms that they don't always live up to it, but they have a sense of something they've inherited as a devotion, as an intention. And that's where we are now.

Remove the Murderer Obama

We have to say, we have to take this city, as I have done,—and I made a decision on this back in October of last year,—and I said, "I'm changing everything, and I'm moving everything back to the center of Manhattan, to Alexander Hamilton and what he represented in his role in the history of the United States." We must

Metropolitan Museum of Art

Alexander Hamilton (1757-1804). This painting, commissioned by merchants of New York City in 1791, was painted by Hamilton's revolutionary compatriot, John Trumbull.

assemble the people inside Manhattan, and also in other parts of the United States, into a single unity of purpose. Unless we can do that, and get rid of Obama, for example, and other afflictions which have been imposed on the United States, we don't have a chance of saving this nation. The very existence of this nation is now in threat, and Obama, the current President Obama, is the chief source of that threat right now. *This is a man who must be absolutely thrown out of office now. He's committed crimes beyond imagination.* He must be removed! All the evidence is available. But we have gutless members of the Congress who don't have the ability to mobilize themselves to a moral decision to recreate and maintain the United States.

Now the United States is not just one thing. The United States is something which contains within it a promise of a better life for other parts of the world, especially for Europe. Europe was sodden with the crime of its own characteristics, some of it not known. Other nations have come up out of it, in Asia, Africa, and parts of South America. They've come up as places that can become the locations of a new development throughout the planet. And that's what we have to do.

But we have to say, start in one place. Here we are: we're taking up a discussion in Manhattan. We know that this role of Manhattan contains within it, within its valuable parts, precisely those sparks with which we can save this nation, and thus, in that way, contribute to the salvation of mankind more generally. And that should be a conscience-stricken view of what stands before us right now.

EIRContents

www.larouchepub.com Volume 42, Number 45, November 13, 2015

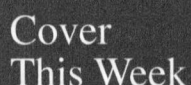

Cover This Week

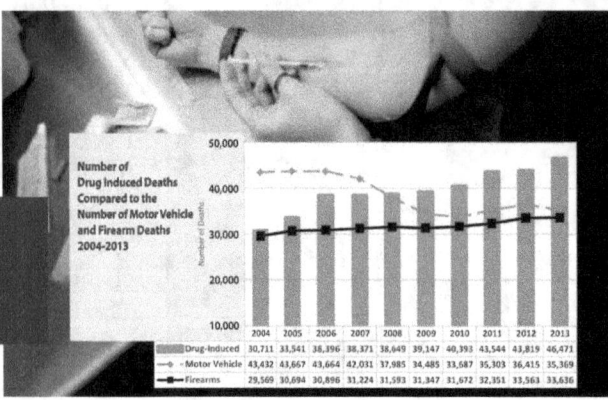

The DEA's 2015 Drug Threat Assessment documents the fact that drug overdose deaths (death by poisoning) began to exceed those from motor vehicles and firearms, starting under Bush, and accelerating under Obama.

The Peace Dividend of the New Silk Road: Global Reconstruction of The Physical Economy

by Alexander Hartmann

Nov. 6—In her webcast of Nov. 4, 2015, the Chair-woman of Germany's Civil Rights Movement Solidarity Party (BüSo) Helga Zepp-LaRouche, emphasized the great crisis, but also the great opportunity, which is presented by the current international situation: "There are two fundamental processes in motion. One is that the trans-Atlantic world is collapsing at a rapid rate—in fact, in America as much as Europe. And at the same time there are very hopeful developments—from China, from the BRICS countries; even the developments in Syria are taking a positive course. It is very difficult to say which direction is currently stronger. This is one of those historical moments where there are objective conditions for either trend to win out—either for the collapse, or for optimistic changes. And everything, or almost everything, in such a situation depends on the subjective factor: are there enough people who grasp the opportunity at hand—or not?"

Zepp-LaRouche referenced a recent conference on the New Silk Road in Madrid: "There the leader of the most important Chinese development agency used the image of the Silk Road being a potential 'Noah's Ark' for all the states in the world who need it. I have picked up on this and somewhat modified it, with the idea that development is the only way we can bring peace to the Middle East, and that a lasting solution can actually only be reached with the concept of 'Peace Through Development.'"

This idea has already been put on the international agenda, because, at the recent Vienna Conference on Syria, China proposed a four-point plan for solving the Syria crisis, "and the fourth point was that the recon-struction process in Syria should begin *immediately* in the regions which have already seen peace, so that the warring parties can see the benefits of the peace divi-dend."

Xinhua/Liu Xiang

Chinese Vice Foreign Minister Li Baodong upon arrival at the multilateral ministerial meeting on Syria in Vienna, Austria, Oct. 30, 2015.

This is precisely the idea of the New Silk Road, "which is already emerging in various ways, from China through Central Asia into Europe, if we extend it into the Middle East." For example, China is building a huge development corridor through Pakistan to the Per-sian Gulf, in which it has invested 46 billion dollars. There are similar efforts beginning in Afghanistan, where China, as well as Russia, has proposed very im-portant programs for development of the country.

"And for a long time we have proposed that the whole Near and Middle East, i.e. the whole of South-west Asia, be considered one region, and that a kind of Marshall Plan be put on the agenda," Zepp-LaRouche said. "That would be a great success, and there are many people who are thinking seriously about it. Be-cause we must ask ourselves: The point is not merely to end the war in Syria, but 'What should the world look like 50 or 100 years from now?'"

The Looming Dangers

But Zepp-LaRouche also alluded to the danger if we do not follow the path of reconstruction:

"We currently have to deal with a mass migration, thus a massive immigration, so to speak, a migration movement similar to that of the mass migration of the old Germanic tribes at the end of the Roman Empire—i.e., it is a movement coming from Africa and from Southwest Asia which simply will not end, because an old order is collapsing, and it is still continuing to collapse."

If you want to stop these many people who are fleeing from war and destitution from becoming an "explosive force" in Europe, "then we must urgently correct the mistakes which the West as a whole has made over the last decades. And that was to deliver these countries over completely to interests other than those actually implementing a development policy. That mistake we must urgently correct."

There are many countries in the world which are thinking in this direction—the BRICS countries and many countries in South America and Asia—"who see a solution in this perspective. And I believe that the Silk Road idea is gradually beginning—in Germany, in France, in Great Britain, in Spain—to gain a foothold as a potential solution. From that I conclude: We have the solution, potentially; we must only move on it."

The Breakdown Crisis in America

The United States also finds itself in a "classical breakdown crisis." As an example, Zepp-LaRouche cited a report in the Nov. 2 *New York Times* on a study which found that the death rate of 40-50 year olds in the United States over the last ten years had risen by about 10 percent—and for people who qualify as poor, actually 22 percent. The most important causes of death

The Drug Enforcement Administration's latest report makes it official: Drug overdoses kill more than motor vehicle accidents or firearms.

were drugs, alcohol, and suicide; the underlying reason lies in the increasing impoverishment of the population and the worsening of health care. Between 2011 and 2014 heroin consumption has risen over 150%—especially because many people are taking heroin as a substitute for much more expensive pain killers. In cities such as New York City, 60% of the population is poor.

"The whole country is really in a breakdown crisis which is absolutely unbelievable," Zepp-LaRouche said. "And I believe that people who realize this, must understand that it is not America as a nation which is behind these wars in the Middle East, or behind all the other things which people blame America for. We are dealing with an empire which destroys *all* nations—including the United States. And as long as this empire has not been effectively defeated, this process will proceed."

Zepp-LaRouche cited the upcoming Paris Climate Conference (COP21) as an example of the policy of this empire. "Of course climate change takes place; of course conditions in certain parts of the earth change; it becomes warmer, the sea level rises to some extent. But, as in earlier periods, mankind must adapt to such developments using modern technology. That is totally feasible because man is the creature which deals with such problems, as before, with scientific and technological progress, and we are a species which can solve all problems scientifically and technologically. It is only a question of time, a question of focus, of how much energy will be applied, how much labor power. Fundamentally, there is no single problem that we, as humanity, can not solve."

But to that end, the common good must be the central focus, and not the profits of an ever richer class, as today, when 80 people own exactly the same amount of wealth as 3.5 billion people. And that is the problem—that we have a world order which caters to speculation, to the maximum profit for a small upper class, to which many people naturally attach themselves because they want to have a part in it—but two billion people don't have enough to eat.... We need a return to a financial and economic policy which puts mankind in the center, and fortunately, it is to some degree already on the way."

As a further example of the paradigm which must be overcome, Zepp-LaRouche cited the West's confrontation policy against Russia: "As long as we don't change this paradigm, we are sitting on a powderkeg, the possible outbreak of a Third World War. Therefore it should actually be absolutely clear: The German government must be challenged forcefully not only to distance itself from this policy, but to make it clear, with concrete steps, that it is not part of such a policy, and that we must immediately and unilaterally lift the sanctions against Russia."

These sanctions in any case are hurting the German economy more than Russia, "and by the way, the German government has already realized that Russia is acting very, very much in Germany's interests by acting against terrorism in Syria, and thereby carrying out the only possible policy which can solve the refugee crisis. In return, it really is time to end the sanctions immediately, and thereby give a clear signal for all Europe: We are not interested in a war against Russia or China, or against anyone."

A Development Perspective on the Agenda

"We must act so that this development perspective comes on the agenda not only for the Middle East and Africa," Helga Zepp-LaRouche stressed. The United States and Europe also need large-scale reconstruction programs. The United States needs a continental high-speed rail system, such as is currently being built in China. This could be linked to the idea of building new cities—science cities, "which at the same time will be cultural and scientific centers which will feature beauty again. We can build beautiful buildings, beautiful cities."

Schiller Institute

A view of the Russian Science City Dubna, taken by a delegation of the Schiller Institute which visited the area Oct. 26 to 30 this year. A 15 minute video on the trip can be seen here.

This effort must be combined "with urgently required water projects, in order to fight the expanding desert in all the U.S. states west of the Mississippi." We can retool the whole military-industrial complex for this purpose, and devote it to the reconstruction of the United States. As a result no one would lose anything, but the whole country would experience a tremendous advantage."

The same thing obviously could be done in Europe as well. "Southern Europe, the Balkans, southern Italy, Spain, and Portugal urgently need a reconstruction program such as we have already presented in 2012. Germany has a deficit of investment in infrastructure—roads, bridges, and so forth—of about 2 trillion Euros, which is not a small amount." The same applies to public housing construction and many other aspects.

This kind of buildup is exactly what China's President Xi Jinping has described as a "win-win perspective:" a perspective from which all countries who collaborate on this model of cooperation, profit. "In other words: We can actually begin to implement a reconstruction program similar to that of the German economic miracle after World War II, and thus gradually solve all our problems, and mankind will have a future. It must simply be put on the agenda. I am optimistic that we can accomplish this, and I also appeal to you: Don't sit like a little bird on the fence of history, as a spectator, but join with us today, and mobilize for these solutions!"

This article has been translated from German.

How Obama Has Destroyed This Country

The following is the transcript of the Nov. 6, 2015 LaRouche PAC webcast.

Matthew Ogden: Good evening. It's Nov. 6, 2015. My name is Matthew Ogden, and you're watching our weekly broadcast here from larouchepac.com of our international Friday night webcast. I'm joined in the studio tonight by Jeffrey Steinberg of *Executive Intelligence Review*, as well as Megan Beets of the LaRouche PAC Science and Research Team.

Now, the three of us did have a chance to meet with Helga and Lyndon LaRouche just a few hours ago; so that has definitely informed the content of the broadcast that you'll hear tonight. What you will hear tonight is a thorough exposition of the continually building case for immediate legal action to be taken against the murderous policies of the Barack Obama Presidency. The case against him continues to snowball.

You'll hear about the media censorship that was ordered directly from the Obama White House to eliminate any coverage in the leading newspapers of record of the United States, including the *Washington Post* and the *New York Times*, of the damning story that was broken by Glenn Greenwald and Jeremy Scahill in *The Intercept*, of the so-called "Drone Papers,"—which expose the lurid details of Obama's weekly kill sessions, which have routinely resulted in innumerable innocent civilian deaths.

You'll hear about the most recent revelations in the case of the bombardment of the Doctors Without Borders hospital in Kunduz, Afghanistan, by which it is now revealed that doctors and other medical personnel who were fleeing the hospital, fleeing the bombardment of this medical facility, were systematically gunned down by U.S. military gunships. This is further building the case that this is indeed an intentional targeting of a medical facility, and amounts to nothing less than a war crime.

You'll hear about the hundreds of thousands of refugees who have been fleeing the illegal wars that have been perpetrated by the Obama Administration in the Middle East and northern Africa, resulting in the massive social displacement of entire portions of these populations as well as widespread death and destruction, as Obama continues to lend his support to the overthrow by radical jihadists of sitting sovereign governments in this region.

You'll hear about the shocking statistics of the rise in the death rates, rising dramatically throughout the United States, particularly among the former skilled, industrial and manufacturing labor force, who were sacrificed at the altar of the bail-out of the bankrupt Wall Street banks by first, the Bush, and now the Obama Administrations. One of the leading causes of this increase in death rates across the United States, and especially in this formerly productive sector of the American labor force, is an unbelievable surge in deaths from heroin and related drug overdoses. This is occurring not only among the inner city minority populations, but also now among suburban middle and upper class white populations, surpassing automobile and firearms rates of mortality and now reaching an epidemic level as characterized by the Centers of Disease Control.

Capitol Hill Forum Hears Warnings of Nuclear War

And finally, you'll hear about the continuing mounting danger of global extinction warfare as the Obama Administration continues to attempt to provoke World War III confrontations with both Russia and China.

Now, this final item was the explicit discussion at a landmark event that occurred this past Wednesday (Nov. 4) on Capitol Hill, which I personally had the opportunity to attend and to be an eyewitness to. This extraordinary event was set up as an informal hearing by Rep. John Conyers, the ranking member of the House

Hearing convenor Rep. John Conyers (D-Mich), dean of the U.S. House of Representatives, speaking at a reception by the Haiti Advocacy Working Group at the Capitol in January 2012.

Reagan's Ambassador to the Soviet Union Jack Matlock, speaking in Sept. 2014 to the Robert S. Strauss Center for International Security and Law.

Judiciary Committee and the dean of the House of Representatives—the longest-serving member of Congress on the House side.

Also in attendance were a number of other Congressmen, including Reps. Barbara Lee, Alan Grayson, Charlie Rangel, Sheila Jackson Lee, and Congressman Walter Jones, among others. The distinguished members of the panel at this informal hearing were all founders of the recently re-established American Committee for East-West Accord, including: former U.S. Ambassador Jack Matlock, who was ambassador to the Soviet Union under President Ronald Reagan; NYU Professor Stephen Cohen; and John Pepper, a leading businessman and former CEO of Proctor & Gamble.

The subject of this hearing was none other than the fact that the Obama policies are on the verge of provoking a thermonuclear confrontation with Russia—a subject which was explicitly presented in those terms— and the fact that without a drastic change in U.S.-Russian relations which must be induced, there is no way that this World War III confrontation can be avoided.

The invitation to this event, which was published by the Committee on East-West Accord and was circulated by the office of Congressman John Conyers, read in part as follows:

> The Ukrainian crisis represents a low in U.S.-Russia relations not seen since the fall of the Soviet Union. And the recent Russian involvement in the Syrian situation is now making the

danger even worse. American and Russian jets flying bombing missions in close proximity to one another, raises the possibility of a military accident between two nuclear-armed powers.

As the *New York Times* warned, the complicated and shifting landscape of alliances leaves us "edging closer to an all-out proxy war between the United States and Russia."

The majority of Americans never lived through the Cuban Missile Crisis of 1962 or the darkest days of the Cold War. They have led lives without the looming specter of nuclear war, but the areas of conflict between our nations are growing. The conflict in Ukraine, the expansion of NATO, Russia's involvement in Syria, and other lesser issues are driving a new wedge between the US and Russia.

While most would agree that conflict between the United States and Russia benefits no one, the likelihood of such a conflict, as well as the serious consequences that it would bring, is not being discussed on Capitol Hill.

Worse Than the Cuban Missile Crisis

Now each member of this panel, and a number of the Congressmen each in their own way, referred to the darkest days of the Cold War, which they all remembered, being senior statesmen of this country. John Conyers and Jack Matlock, who was an ambassador and a close collaborator of President Ronald Reagan,

Professor of Russian Studies Stephen Cohen, at the Russian Center in New York City in Oct. 2012.

both referred to the Cuban Missile Crisis. They recalled the experience of "duck and cover," hiding under one's desk, nuclear air raid drills, underground bomb shelters, nuclear bunkers, and stated that although the situation at that time seemed bad, the situation today is as bad, or worse. They added that unless the direct provocations against Russia are halted, there is very real possibility which exists of open nuclear warfare breaking out, and exterminating the human race.

Ambassador Matlock echoed much of what he had stated during previous appearances in Washington, D.C., but also especially during his recent appearance on the same dais as President Vladimir Putin at the Valdai discussion club in Sochi, Russia two weeks ago. Matlock elaborated the 20-year process of broken promises and outright lies and deceptions that resulted in the eastward expansion of NATO all the way up to Russia's borders, which has an immediate and calculated threat to Russia's domestic security, worse, in fact, as Matlock pointed out, than the Berlin crisis of 1961. The fact is that Berlin was not directly on Russia's borders, but now you have the immediate proximity of Ukraine, and other countries right on the borders of Russian territory.

One More Base…

Stephen Cohen underscored Matlock's remarks and warned point-blank, in no uncertain terms, that the placement of one more base on Russia's borders, or the incorporation of one more country in Eastern Europe into the NATO security alliance, military alliance, would mean war between the U.S. and Russia, and everything that entails.

He pointed out that former Obama Ambassador to Russia Michael McFaul's blog has shifted from what he called "Mickey Mouse democracy promotion" to now, all-out strident calls for outright warfare and regime change provocations. Cohen emphasized that the danger of war today is far worse than at any time during the Cold War, mostly because of this cross-partisan 100% close-to-consensus when it comes to the demonization of Putin and Russia, and the lack of any substantial pushback from among the corridors of power in Washington, against this narrative, especially from within Congress.

This failure was something which, he noted, was changing with this historic event, changing in front of the eyes of all those who attended this event. It had a packed audience, standing-room only, and was the first open discussion of this kind in a forum such as this by *anyone* on Capitol Hill.

The Real Enemy

And finally, John Pepper made a very impassioned call for a completely new paradigm in U.S.-Russia relations, one which is founded on a concept of common security, and a creation of a mutual common security architecture, against what he identified as the *real* enemies, as opposed to the made-up enemies: the real enemies of both the United States and of Russia. Number one: international terrorism, and ISIS, in specific. And number two: what he identified as the greatest enemy of all mankind, which is thermonuclear warfare itself. He stated, the true enemy that we must guard ourselves against is the enemy of nuclear annihilation, and I think we can all find common cause in that.

So, as I said, this was really an extraordinary event, especially when you juxtapose it to another event which was happening literally simultaneously on Capitol Hill, just a few doors down from this hearing room. And this was a hearing featuring none other than [Assistant Secretary of State for European and Eurasian Affairs] Victoria Nuland herself, and that counterposition was pointed out very clearly by numerous participants in this event, both members of the panel, and members of the audience, as representative of the two stark choices that are facing the American people right now: Obama's World War III and thermonuclear annihilation, or a new international policy of cooperation and partnership with Russia, as well as with China. Which means the immediate end of the murderous and deadly policies of the Obama Administration.

So, with that said, I'd like to ask Jeff Steinberg to come to the podium for the next segment of tonight's broadcast, to elaborate a little bit more on what I've just covered.

What the Capitol Hill Forum Fatally Left Out

Jeff Steinberg: Thanks, Matt. There were obviously some important things that were said during that John Conyers event on Wednesday afternoon up on Capitol Hill, but I think it's critical to recognize that there was one thing that was *not* said, and that was that the only viable solution is the removal of President Obama through either impeachment, or invoking of the

---

Hillary is Part of Obama's Team

Nov 9—Hillary is part of the Obama team. That's it; that's what has to be said. She's part of the Obama team, and has been ever since she began lying for the sake of Obama. Remember when she supported Obama's illegal Libya war in 2011? Remember her gushing praise for the torture-murder of Libyan President Qaddafi that October, on Obama's orders? When Obama murdered Muammar Qaddafi, Lyndon LaRouche said that Obama would go for war in Syria next, on the way to a global nuclear war. Just what has happened.

Hillary is part of the Obama team. Say it! That will help accelerate the coming O'Malley torrent.

The point is, she's always lied, and she's lied on the basis of covering for Obama. And everything has been in that form. We know that she's a stooge for Obama,—a chronic stooge for a liar. Obama is a liar, and so Hillary's a liar. Why is she a liar? Because she's working for Obama!

Hillary is a lying lawyer. She has consistently lied for Obama,—ever since his illegal war on Libya.

Twenty-fifth Amendment, or some combination of actions, as happened with Richard Nixon, to force his immediate resignation.

The fact of the matter is that you had prominent American diplomats, prominent American scholars, leading members of Congress, standing there, and saying to the American people that the President of the United States is pushing the world towards thermonuclear annihilation, and yet nobody took it to the logical conclusion, which is that we've got to get this guy out of office.

Now, in our discussion earlier today with Lyn and Helga LaRouche, Mr. LaRouche was reflecting on where we stand, in terms of the dangers represented to, really, the survival of the entire trans-Atlantic region. Because that's really what's on the table right now. Assuming we even avoid the immediate threat of thermonuclear war and annihilation, the simple fact is that if the current trendlines continue, without a reversal, in a very short period of time the entire trans-Atlantic region will be doomed, will be finished, will not resemble anything like what Europe and the United States historically represented, particularly the United States.

Parts of South America may very well survive, because they're already aligning themselves with the Asia-Pacific region, and with Eurasia more broadly, where countries like China, India, Russia are doing relatively well compared to the complete breakdown process that's inflicted the entire trans-Atlantic region.

Now the problem of not directly addressing the clear and obvious solution to this crisis, namely the constitutional removal of President Obama from office, is in fact indicative of a much deeper problem, a problem that very few people other than people such as Mr. LaRouche think about constantly.

The bottom line is that since the very beginning of the Twentieth Century, since the intervention by Lord Bertrand Russell and others around him to destroy Classical science, and to replace it with mathematics and with the disease of pragmatism—since that process began at the beginning of the Twentieth Century— we've been on a steady downward trajectory—culturally, economically, philosophically, morally. We've been, throughout the trans-Atlantic region, in a slow but now intensifying complete collapse of society, and when you broach the issue of a President who has committed atrocities, such as his drone kill policy, all you need to do, is go back on the LaRouche PAC website, and review the last three Friday evening webcasts. You'll have all of the details you need to know about that.

The fact that there has not been a move to remove this President from office, is because the disease of pragmatism has infected our political institutions to such a great degree, and has infected our general population to an even greater degree, that the only measure that can prevent the possible annihilation of mankind, is considered to be "unpractical, it's not pragmatic, there's no guarantee that this process will succeed."

So, we've been on this long trajectory downward. It's very much like the principle of how you boil a frog. If you put a pot of water on the stove, and get that water boiling to a full boil, and try to throw the frog in the boiling water, the frog's going to jump right out. He'll run away and you'll never find him. If you put the frog in a pot of warm water, comfortably warm water, and have a low flame, then, gradually, that water will reach a boiling point, and the frog won't notice it, because the incremental changes are gradual. That's why you've got to look back and consider where we are as a trans-Atlantic civilization today, and ask yourself, from that standpoint: can we survive by continuing to cling to pragmatism and avoid taking the necessary urgent measures that can save us from otherwise certain doom?

Don't Call Obama a Murderer, or You'll Be Next

The drone policy, as Mr. LaRouche emphasized in our discussion today, is emblematic of Obama. He's a mass killer. He *boasted* to White House staff, back in 2011, that he was really good at killing. Coming into the office of the Presidency, he had *no idea* how good he was at targeting people to be killed by others. But that's the character of it; that's what the "Drone Papers," like the "Pentagon Papers" which earlier brought down Richard Nixon, show.

The "Drone Papers" alone are more than sufficient to bring down President Obama. But it has not yet happened, because a few phone calls from the White House to the *New York Times*, to the *Washington Post*, got the word out: this story is taboo; it's not practical to tell the truth about this mass murderer, because we might get cut off from access to the White House. So, you've got this phenomenon.

You have the new reports that Matt just mentioned concerning the bombing of the Doctors Without Borders [MSF] hospital in Kunduz, providing more and more evidence that it was a pre-meditated assault on an international medical facility under the lamest of excuses, and that as doctors and nurses and patients were fleeing, they were being shot, on the grounds that any-

youtube

Doctors Without Borders General-Director Christopher Stokes, at the news conference Nov. 5 where he exposed the U.S. Airforce's deliberate targetting of medical personnel at the hospital in Kunduz.

body who was there was automatically, *de facto* Taliban, and fair game for another mass kill.

Destruction of Life

But there's many, many more things to consider. You have the conditions of life of the American people, which have been destroyed, systematically, boiling-frog style, over a period of, really, the last 40 years, or you could say even the period going back to the death of Franklin Roosevelt in April of 1945.

It's been a largely downward trajectory ever since then, and that is merely a slice of the process that began right at the turn of the Twentieth Century, with Bertrand Russell's invasion and assault against science. If you look back at the sweep of the Nineteenth Century, you had some of the greatest accomplishments in culture and in science—in real, physical science. You had Bernhard Riemann, you had the great classical composers—Beethoven, Brahms. You had the work of Friedrich Schiller, branching over from the 1700s into the 1800s. You had a renaissance underway, particularly in Europe, particularly in Germany, during the end of the Nineteenth Century, covering the whole sweep of that Century. And suddenly, it came it came to a screeching halt, with the British top-down intervention, personified by Bertrand Russell. And we've been on a cultural downslide ever since. If you destroy the culture, you destroy the moral fabric of a society.

So, where are we now? Earlier today, as I'm sure many of you are aware, a series of propagandistic lies were put out by the Bureau of Labor Statistics, saying that 271,000 jobs were created last month in the United States, and that the unemployment rate is now officially down to 5%. Five percent unemployment is considered to be tantamount to full employment.

Well, those figures are an absolute lie, and I think if any of you think about it, any of you watching this broadcast now, think about whether your conditions of life are better or worse than they were at the start of the Obama Presidency, or, even more so, at the end of the Clinton Presidency, when Bush and Cheney came in. If you say, "My conditions are better, my prospects for my children and grandchildren are better," then you are in an extremely small minority. The simple reality is that half of the 271,000 jobs claimed to have been created, are *purely fictitious*. They're the result of a mathematical sleight-of-hand trick, projecting, on average, death and life rates and starts of new businesses and bankruptcies. But there's nothing normal about the current economy. So, forget that number!

If you take the fact that 94 million working-age Americans, qualified to be in the labor force, are *not* counted as part of the labor force, because they are either chronically unemployed or have never been able to find a job, then if you add those 94 million people, working-age people, in, you find that the actual unemployment rate in the United States, is 23%! That number is on a par with the worst, darkest, days of the Great Depression in the 1930s, before Roosevelt put people back to work.

U.S. Mortality Rates *Rise*

A study came out just this past week from Princeton University, indicating that for the first time in a long time, there are more and more Americans dying during their middle-age—their 40s and 50s. And this is due to a combination of job loss, of lack of access to adequate medical care, addiction to drugs and alcohol—again, a reflection of a process of chronic unemployment or under-employment. In rural United States, according to a report in the *New York Times* earlier this week, the rate of suicides is rising astronomically.

In a few moments, Megan will give you a detailed readout on the fact that we're in the midst of a heroin epidemic in the United States, and it's mostly afflicting middle-class and upper middle-class households all over the country. You have all of the signs there, as if anyone out there needed to be reminded or told, about

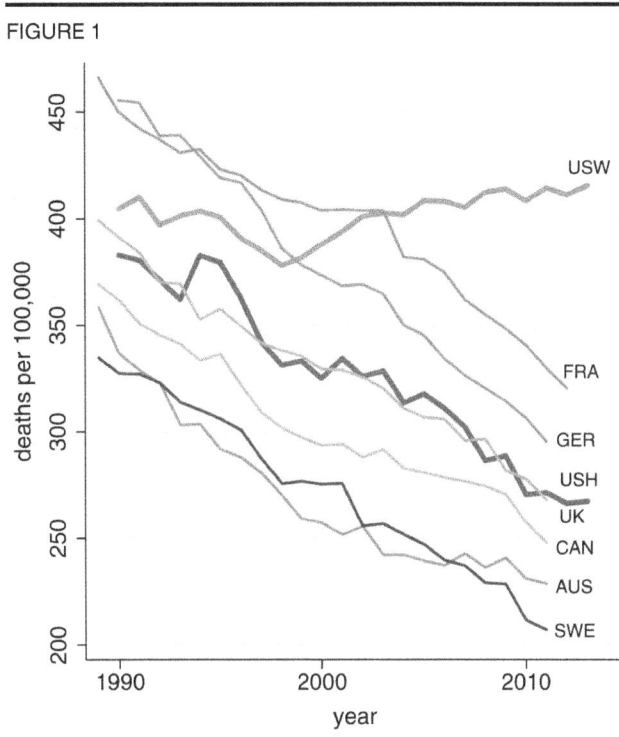

FIGURE 1

The shocking rise of mortality rates among U.S. White non-Hispanics (USW), ages 45-54, shown in the study "Rising morbidity and mortality in midlife among white non-Hispanic Americans in the 2st century," by Anne Case and Angus Deaton, published in the Proceedings of the National Academy of Sciences. *These rates are compared with U.S. Hispanics (USH), and six comparison countries: France (FRA), Germany (GER), the United Kingdom (UK), Canada (CAN), Australia (AUG), and Sweden (SWE). The full report can be found here.*

the actual collapse of the conditions of life.

So, this has occurred during the period of the Bush-Cheney Administration and during the period of Obama. There's nothing that we can do right now in particular about Bush and Cheney, from the standpoint that they're out of office. They should have been impeached for a whole range of reasons, and they were not impeached. Yet President Obama is the current President. And he stands guilty of crimes that even go beyond the scope of what Bush and Cheney did. The drone killing policy is a policy of mass murder.

In effect, you should be thinking about President Obama from the standpoint of somebody who is a bigger mass murderer than Charles Manson. How would you feel about having Charles Manson in the White House? Well, guess what? Maybe you do. So, the question is, and this is addressed to the outstanding individuals who did appear at that Congressional forum, and it's also addressed to you, the American people. When are you going to shed the disease of pragmatism and face the reality of the situation that you are now living through? This is not something you watch on television, or read about in the newspapers or on your personal computer. This is the life that you are being subjected to; and there's no reason for it.

The trans-Atlantic region is dead; the U.S. economy is dead. The European economy is even more dead in many areas than the U.S. economy is. Asia is not thriving because of the impact of the trans-Atlantic crisis, but Asia is doing vastly better. There's growth going on—China, India, even Russia; there's growth going on in the entire region. There's a perspective of optimism, about space exploration, about extending the high-speed links from the Asia-Pacific coast on to the Atlantic coast of Europe.

The United States and Europe are living as if on a different planet with a different mindset; and that can and must be broken. And one of the first steps that must be taken is that there's got to be a genuine outpouring that says that this President's got to go, that Wall Street has got to be shut down, because one of the greatest crimes that President Obama has committed has been to be a lackey of Wall Street and the City of London, putting their interests above those of the American people.

So, it's time to wake up to your own condition and do something about it. As I said, there are leading political figures who are scared to death that we are on the cusp of thermonuclear war; they're now talking about it more openly. Don't get me wrong. It's not insignificant that leading American diplomats and members of Congress talked about the fact that we're on the edge of thermonuclear war at a public forum on Capitol Hill.

But how many of you even knew about that before you heard this broadcast tonight? I can assure you, you did not read it on the front page of the *New York Times*, the *Washington Post*, or the *Wall Street Journal*; you didn't hear about it on the six o'clock news. So, it's time to wake up; and those people who are in responsible leading positions have got to stop being pragmatic and pulling their punches. And they've got to join us and join Mr. LaRouche in saying, "We've got an immediate mission. We've got to bring down this Presidency, and we've got to bring down Wall Street."

If you don't do that, then you're not serious about stopping thermonuclear war, and you're not serious about turning around the collapse of the entire trans-Atlantic region.

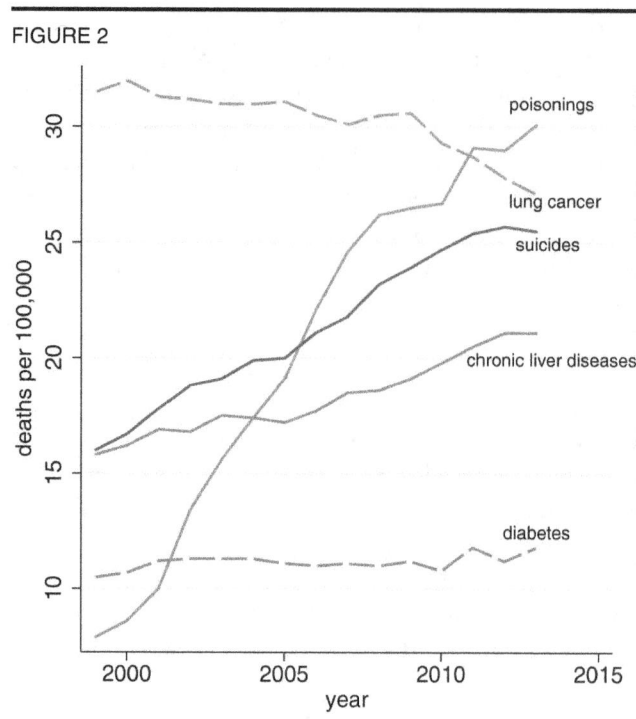

FIGURE 2

The astronomical rise in mortality among the white non-Hispanics ages 45-54, by cause. From the Case/Deaton study.

So, that's the issue on the table. And it was a wonderful event on Wednesday, but this missing ingredient is deadly if it's not actually picked up.

Obama Kills Americans

Megan Beets: So, on the topic of Obama being very good at killing, let's take a closer look at what's been done to the working population of the United States over the course of the Bush and Obama Presidencies. As Jeff mentioned, on Nov. 4, the Drug Enforcement Administration released its 2015 National Drug Threat Assessment Report, which paints a picture similar to one released by the Centers for Disease Control in August: a staggering picture of the drug use and drug overdose increases in the United States, which has risen to epidemic levels under the regimes of Bush and Obama.

The document reports that drug-related deaths, as Matthew mentioned in the opening, drug-related deaths have risen to become the leading cause of injury death in the United States. More than firearms; more than car accidents. And in 2013 alone, the United States lost 46,470 people to drug overdoses—46,000 people. That's more than 120 per day. Now among drugs, controlled pre-

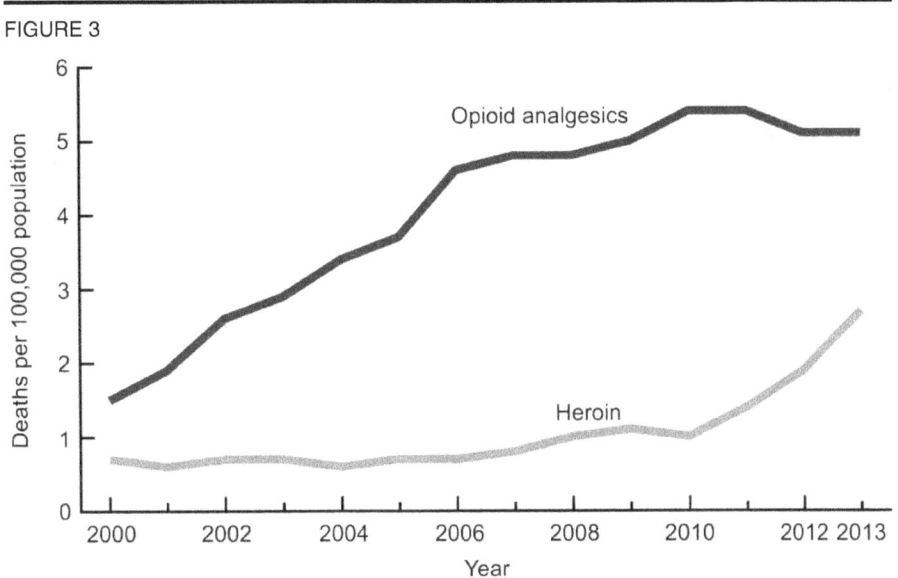

FIGURE 3

CDC/NCHA, National Vital Statistics System, Mortality.

The complementary increase in heroin deaths, as compared to the decrease in deaths from opioid analgesics is shown in this chart, part of a study by the Centers for Disease Control. The data can be found here.

scription drugs—mainly opioids—and heroin, account for the largest type of drug by far; and the slight decline of the use of prescription drugs is being steadily replaced by the use of heroin, as people shift over to what's a much more deadly drug. But it's also much cheaper and much, much more widely available.

Now, to illustrate that a little bit, in 2013 there were 169,000 new users of heroin; many of them very young. Between 2013 and 2014, the rate of current heroin use—in other words, people who have used heroin in the past 30 days—rose by 51%. Between 2007 and 2013—or in other words, during the course of Obama's Presidency—the addiction to heroin rose 150%; and the deaths by overdose of heroin more than tripled.

Now the primary area where this increase of death has occurred, is in the Midwest; the formerly industrial centers that LaRouche took the spearpoint to save over the course of 2005 and the following years, when under the Bush-Cheney Administration, the auto industry and related machine tool sectors were gutted and crushed. Now it's the Midwest, followed closely by New England and the New York/New Jersey area—all of these formerly productive industrial centers of the country which have suffered in every way under Bush and Obama.

Now the increase, as you might guess, for the most part is not concentrated in the inner cities; although I will mention that in the city of Baltimore, one in ten people is a heroin user. The epidemic is not centered among the poorest people in the country; it's centered in the middle class, the working class. For example, families with an income of $50,000 or more, for families of that income rate, heroin addiction has risen by 60% in the last four years. These are working class, upper class families and their children.

But this picture of the epidemic use of drugs is just part of a broader picture. Death is on the rise under President Obama. A study was released just a few weeks ago in September, which is receiving wide coverage this week, which states that since 1999, over the course of the four terms of Bush and Obama, the death rate among middle-aged white Americans in the age range of 45-54 has risen dramatically; in an unprecedented way, 10% overall, and 20% among the poorer, less educated strata.

This increase of the death rate of middle-aged people is not a natural shift in demographics; it's not due to some overall change in disease mortality rates. In fact, for comparison, in comparable industrialized countries around the world, the mortality rate for exactly this class of people has *fallen* by 25% to 30%. So, this is purely the result of a conscious policy in the United States by Bush and Obama.

The leading cause is not disease. The leading causes are signs of the complete degeneration and despair among the American population: drug abuse; alcohol abuse. And in fact, the authors of the report note particularly, heroin and opioid overdoses, and suicide. And as Jeff referenced, in rural areas of the United States, the suicide rates since 2004 have risen by 20%.

So here you have an overview of the stark reality of the Obama death policy, so clearly seen in the attack on the hospital in Afghanistan, turned against the American people. When presented with some of these figures the other day, LaRouche responded with this: He said, "Why didn't we, as a nation, respond years back, and take action to stop this from happening? How did people get set up to accept the economic policies of de-

Creative Commons/Andrew Jameson

Typical of the shutdown of productive industry in the U.S. Midwest is this Fisher Body Plant in Detroit, photographed in 2008.

struction of science, of industry, along with endless bail outs of Wall Street? How were we induced to submit to do this to ourselves?"

So, I'd like to ask Jeff to come to the podium to respond and elaborate.

The Courage to Act

Steinberg: I think it goes back to what I said earlier. Slowly, the level of culture, the level of real science that had permeated our culture even here in the United States in the Nineteenth Century has been under steady and constant assault; largely coming from the British, particularly reflected in people like Lord Bertrand Russell, who wrote books professing to be about science.

Russell wrote a book in 1951, *The Impact of Science on Society*, but he didn't talk about science. He talked about methods of destruction of young minds by turning the education system into a system that basically drives people into accepting their subservience to be trained, to be submissive, to be non-inquisitive. And again, the disease that Russell imposed from the beginning of the Twentieth Century was the disease of replacing physical science with mathematics. Everything comes down to a formula; everything comes down to a probability. If it's not highly probable, then it's not practical, and therefore, don't go there.

So, you've had an assault on education, from the kindergarten level on up, all the way to the major universities professing to be the great halls of advanced educa-

tion. You've had a culture that has been destructive in the most unbelievable and egregious ways. And the net effect is that even compared to the early 1970s, people have lost a certain sense of fight. They'd rather watch reality television. Our leaders have accepted the idea that there are boundary conditions on what they can even dare think about.

Last week on this broadcast, we talked about former Sen. Mike Gravel, who, as a lowly first-term Senator from Alaska, had the audacity to put the Pentagon Papers in the Congressional record. That act in 1971 led to the demise of President Nixon, and contributed mightily to the end of the Vietnam War. So, there are glimmers of recognition among some of our elder statesmen that things used to be different.

And so, we've got an enormous challenge on our hands right now. Do we continue to tolerate, even knowing that the President of the United States is sitting down every Tuesday afternoon with a small group of White House advisors and basically ordering the murder of individual citizens from nations all over the world, some of them American citizens, without any kind of oversight, and without any accountability for his actions?

As Megan just said, he's presided over an invasion of drugs, whether it's over-the-counter prescription or black-market illegal drugs; we have 94 million citizens of working age who are not working in the real economy. Clearly not every one of those people is sleeping under a bridge somewhere. How many of them are directly involved in the black market economy that's shoving heroin at a record rate into the arms of American citizens? It's all of a package.

And again, as I said earlier, and as Mr. LaRouche emphasized in our discussion this afternoon, Obama's got to go, and the book of evidence is absolutely there. It's comprehensive, it's irrefutable. Some of the crimes that he is documented to be guilty of are crimes that go beyond simply the question of impeachment. They may wind up being the basis for criminal prosecution, because the immunity afforded to elected officials does not extend to outright criminal action.

So, we've got Wall Street, that's a parasite sitting on

top of and destroying the United States economy. There are straight-forward measures that could be taken to eliminate Wall Street, starting with the idea of simply re-instating Glass-Steagall. There are many things that could be done. We could issuing credit to rebuild our infrastructure. We could be adopting the model of Franklin Roosevelt from when he first came into office, setting up training programs for young people to give them the necessary skills and to also give them the sense of optimism that they've got a constructive role to play in society, and that they've got a bright future ahead of them.

The crash site of Russia's Flight 9268 in the Sinai Desert, as published on Nov. 2, 2015.

All of these things could be done. They're all right there. If you go to the LaRouche PAC website, you will see there's a massive amount of material spelling out chapter and verse exactly what kinds of measures can and must be taken to turn this situation around. But ultimately it starts with a very subjective question: Are you prepared to fight for your own vital interests? Are you prepared to hold elected officials to a Constitutional standard, and to hold them accountable if they fail to live up to it? These are the issues. These are the questions that are really right now staring us in the face, because we don't have much time left. We don't have a great deal of time to solve these problems, to tackle these issues, and the question is, are you prepared to give up your pragmatism, to turn off your television, and to do something constructive for your country, for your family, and for your future generations?

That's really the issue and that's the question that should be the burning issue on everybody's mind at this moment.

The Downing of Russian Airbus A321M

Ogden: Now, our final segment for this evening is our institutional question, which reads as follows: "Mr. LaRouche, the Russian-operated Airbus A321M crashed last Saturday shortly after taking off from the Red Sea resort of Sharm al-Sheikh, on its way to St. Petersburg, killing all 224 people on board. There are strong but unconfirmed reports that the plane had been downed by a bomb, a claim contested by both Egypt and Russia. British Foreign Secretary Philip Ham-mond, however, said that Britain had weighed the whole information picture, including the Islamic State's claim of responsibility after the crash, and had concluded that there *is* a significant possibility. If these reports are substantiated through examination of the plane wreckage, what actions do you suggest the Russian government should take against the perpetrators of this tragic crime?

Steinberg: First of all, I think the actions taken by the British Foreign Secretary were obnoxious and egregious. The British have no role whatsoever in this investigation. If they had communications intercepts suggesting that terrorists were planning such an attack, then the obvious question is why didn't they inform the Egyptian and Russian authorities, if they knew this was happening? The fact of the matter is that the British basically staged an ambush for Egyptian President el-Sisi, because it was upon his arrival in London for a long-scheduled state visit that Hammond made these comments, and basically announced at the same time that British Airways was suspending flights into Egypt.

So, you've got a British game being played here, and an Obama game, because an unnamed Obama Administration official immediately came out and told Reuters that the United States is in agreement with the British in terms of jumping the gun, and drawing these hasty and perhaps completely false conclusions.

Now, what Mr. LaRouche said is, first of all, you've got to let the Russians conduct the investigation. The Russians are perfectly capable of conducting a thorough and honest and comprehensive forensic investigation to determine what happened. And because of the nature of the area where the crash occurred, namely, in the Sinai desert, all of the remains of the plane have been recovered. The black boxes have been recovered, with a little bit of damage to one of them. All of the bodies by and large have been recovered. And therefore, because you're dealing with people who have competence, and who have a vested interest in finding out what really happened, Mr. LaRouche emphasized, let the Russians do their job. Don't jam them. Don't try to speed it up. Patiently wait for the investigation to be concluded.

And I should say that the head of the Russian FSB, their intelligence service, Alexander Bortnikov, issued a statement today. I'll just read it—it's brief—but it goes very much to the point that Mr. LaRouche just made. Bortnikov said, and it was publicized on Channel 1 TV in Russia today:

We need to obtain absolutely objective and verified data on the reasons for the crash of the plane. This is necessary for purposes of investigating the cause of this disaster, and for informing the public. This work must be done in the most meticulous fashion, taking as much time as may be required, and I want to state that until we determine the actual causes of what happened, I think it is appropriate to halt Russian civil aviation flights to Egypt. This chiefly involves tourism. At the same time, we find it necessary to cooperate actively with the Egyptian authorities in joint work on the investigation of the causes of this disaster.

Russia 1 then quoted the official spokesman for President Putin, Mr. Peskov, who said the President concurred with Bortnikov's recommendations; and he added "Halting the flights does not yet mean that the version that it was an act of terrorism is being viewed as the main one in the investigation of this air disaster. Experts continue to exclude nothing, including the possibility of a bomb explosion onboard the plane." So, this is the beginnings of an investigation into a serious tragedy; 224 people were killed in it. And it's not known yet; we don't have the results of that forensic investigation.

Now as the question of what the Russians should do, I think the answer is, pretty obviously, that they're al-

White House/Pete Souza

President Obama with one of his key advisors on choosing drone victims, CIA Director John Brennan. This photo from Dec. 2012 shows Brennan, then Director of the National Counterterrorism Center, briefing Obama on the Sandy Hook shootings.

ready doing it. The Russians, as of September 30, are carrying out a systematic, targetted campaign against the terrorist networks that are operating inside Syria. They are, at the same time, aggressively pursuing a diplomatic track to try to bring an end to this five-year horror inside Syria; and that will obviously have major implications for the situation next door in Iraq, in Lebanon, in other parts of the entire Middle East region. So, in effect, Putin already made a command decision and launched the flanking operation against the Islamic State and allied jihadist groups and their sponsors in countries like Saudi Arabia, Qatar, and Turkey.

So, it would be a mistake to veer off what is already an extremely effective and ongoing flanking operation. If it turns out—and again, it's premature to make any judgement on this—but if does turn out that the Islamic State or some affiliate or spin-off was involved in planting a bomb on that plane, then that's another story; and you've got to carry it several steps further. What was the infrastructure through which that operation was conducted, if it proves to have been a bomb rather than a mechanical failure? Now, if you're talking about the Islamic State, if you're talking about Nusra, if you're talking about al-Qaeda, then ultimately, face it; you're talking about operations that were allowed to grow and allowed to fester as a result of the policies of the Bush and now Obama Presidencies, and the Blair and Cameron governments in Britain.

So, ultimately, all roads lead back to what we've been discussing throughout the entire evening broadcast tonight; namely, as the former head of the Defense Intelligence Agency [DIA], Gen. Mike Flynn, told al-Jazeera, and has subsequently repeated in interviews with American and Russian media: the President, the administration were warned that the actions that the United States was taking in places such as Benghazi, was fueling the growth of jihadist organizations. And it was not an oversight, or that the warnings were ignored, as General Flynn said, it was in pursuit of the ongoing current policy that they made a willful decision to keep doing what they were doing, having been fully informed that this was fueling the growth of not just al-Qaeda. But back in 2012, DIA was already looking at the prospects of the creation of a jihadist caliphate in the area on the territory of parts of Iraq and Syria.

So, in other words, the [former] head of the DIA has said openly and publicly President Obama willfully pursued a policy that created ISIS. So, let me ask you, if—and we're not there yet by any means—but if it turns out that this was a bomb; if it turns out that the Islamic State was involved in it, then let's go higher up the political and logistical chain of command. Are we not talking about the consequences of Bush and Obama administration policies and certainly the policies of the parallel British government?

So, that's another dimension of what I want you to think about this evening. And I hope that you've been disturbed enough by what we've discussed tonight that you'll lose a bit of sleep and think about what's required to end the tyranny of pragmatism. To end the tyranny of basically "go along to get along;" and what it will take to actually solve these crises before they bring the entire trans-Atlantic region down, or may ultimately lead to thermonuclear annihilation.

Ogden: So, as I said at the outset of this broadcast, the evidence has continued to accumulate. The case against Obama has now begun to snowball; the avalanche is ready to begin. It is now incumbent on those who are in responsible positions of leadership to take the legal and Constitutional actions which must be taken to protect the American people and to protect the people of the entire world from the deadly consequences of the continuation of the policies of the Obama Presidency.

Phoenix Project Syria: Discussion Points on the Reconstruction of Syria

by Ulf Sandmark and Hussein Askary, *EIR*

Stockholm, Oct. 16—The following "Discussion Points on the Reconstruction of Syria" were prepared after discussions with Syrian government authorities. The Swedish association the Syrian Support Committee for Democracy visited several government ministries and authorities in Damascus, December 2014. EIR Stockholm correspondent Ulf Sandmark participated in the delegation's week-long visit to Syria. See "Will the West take the road to Damascus?" Hussein Askary is the editor for the EIR *Arabic language edition. This document is available in Arabic there.*

Stockholm, October 16—**Why discuss reconstruction in the midst of a devastating war?**

Hope makes Man human. The Hope for reconstruction mobilizes the creative powers of Man, and is what puts his soul closest to The Creator.

By elevating the eyes to the vision of postwar reconstruction and development, the Syrian nation can demonstrate in the clearest way its view of Man in contrast to the evil and meaningless destruction personified by its enemies. This will be obvious not only to ourselves and the world, but not the least to those enemies who can think, convincing them that their warfare will not lead to something better for themselves. A reconstruction plan will show those enemies that they would have a better future cooperating with the Syrian government than by continuing their warfare.

The Hope for the future of Syria is its most powerful weapon against the pessimism, desperation, and inhumanity of the enemy.

Who Has Hope and Who Does Not?

The BRICS (Brazil, Russia, India, China, South Africa) has brought half of mankind into an organization dedicated to a paradigm of development and prosperity for themselves and the world. The BRICS has finally put a strong organized force behind the hopes expressed by the Third World in their Bandung conference, the Non-Allied Movement, and the Group of 77, to lift the world out of poverty and colonialism.

In contrast to Syria and the BRICS, the Western world is dominated by its globalized financial system that offers no hope. Of the two quadrillions of U.S. dollars in paper value, more than 90% represent specula-

FIGURE 1

Linking Syria to the New Silk Road

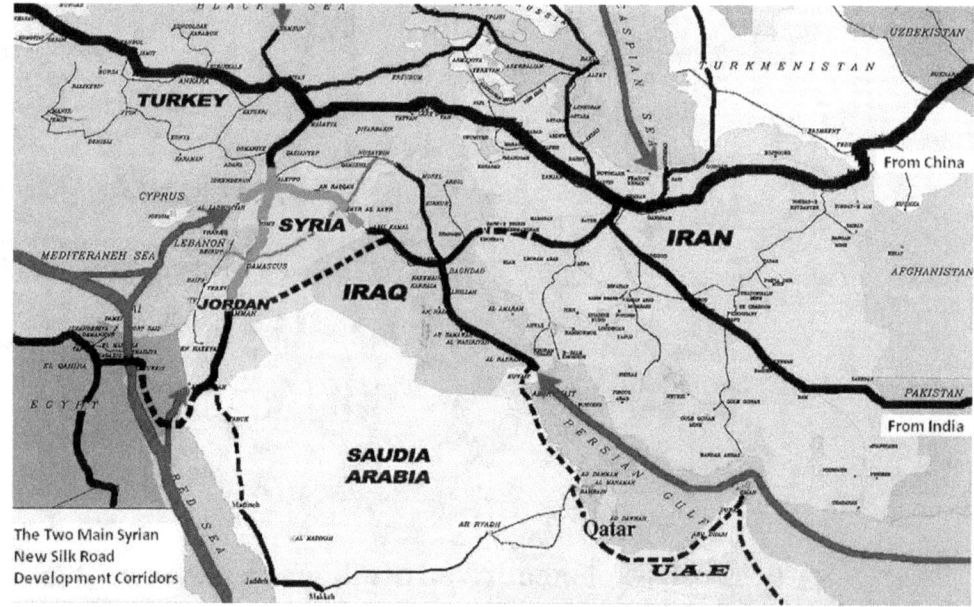

The Two Main Syrian New Silk Road Development Corridors

Ulf Sandmark/adapted from a map by the International Railway Union

The magenta "crossroads" shown in Syria, depict the authors' vision of how that war-torn nation can be linked up with already existing and planned (dotted) Silk Road routes.

tive debts. This is a financial pyramid game without comparison in world history, and has only been kept afloat by unending capital injections from Central banks and state budgets. The desperate condition of the Western financial system has pressured Western politicians into allowing massive financial looting of its citizens and the real economy.

The looting is exemplified by the Greek crisis, but has had a much more devastating impact on the Third World. It is not as easy for the Western banks to loot the BRICS nations any more. The method for imposing the looting and domination over the BRICS and other independent nations is the destabilization and chaos that terrorists and regional wars can spread into all of Central Asia, China, India, and Russia to break the resistance and leadership of these major nations.

SANA
Electrical workers at work in the suburbs of Damascus. Repairing the electricity grid will be a major task of reconstruction.

Syria is on the front lines of this policy called geopolitics, which is the method of the old British Empire to suppress competing and emerging world powers. Since the United States currently supports this British geopolitical doctrine, the threat of use of the U.S. nuclear weapons is included in the extortion method against the BRICS nations—which puts the world on the brink of an immediate total catastrophe.

It is the desperation and lack of hope in the Western financial system and the old colonial powers, which are projected against Syria and other war-torn nations, in the form of terrorism and the policy of regime change. What would fundamentally halt the policy of war is a solution for the financial crisis, with a banking reform and a restart of the physical economies of the Western world.

These proposals have been put forward by the American statesman Lyndon LaRouche and his wife Helga Zepp-LaRouche and the Schiller Institutes internationally. Many Western politicians are now pursuing these same proposals to solve the financial crisis. The strongest hope for the world is the immense push by the BRICS nations for a new paradigm for world development. Together these forces still have the possibility of turning Europe and the United States away from the policy of war. The heroic resistance of the Syrian Arab Republic against the imperial forces is therefore part of a both military and economic struggle. It unifies the peoples of the whole world in the hope and struggle for a new just economic world order.

How Can Reconstruction Be Financed When The Nation Has Been Ruined By War?

The freedom Syria is struggling for is to establish thefoundation for the Syrian economy and its right to create credit and money. The people, the land, and the country's natural resources have a huge potential. With a reconstruction and development plan an even greater potential is created.

A farmer or an entrepreneur will need credit from someone else to realize his potential. A free nation can make its own decisions to realize its potential. It can do that by deciding to give itself credit, using its own future productivity as the security for the credit. For this a special financial system called a "Hamiltonian credit system" is needed.

The starting point for a credit system is a vision for reconstruction. Optimally it will include a development plan declaring step by step what the nation intends to have accomplished at defined future dates. With this plan as the foundation, the government can issue the necessary credit to put all the available workforce, tools, and materials to work. The government or its authority gives the permission for projects to start and at the same time provides for the credits. The projects can be run by either private entrepreneurs or government authorities.

For the issuing of this reconstruction credit, the government needs an institution devoted to the rebuilding of the nation, such as a National Bank or a special new Reconstruction Bank. The nation of Syria can raise the capital for this bank in a way similar to the way Egypt mobilized its people to finance the Suez canal: by issuing stock offerings directly to the citizens of Syria at home or in the diaspora.

By these means, the Reconstruction Bank will have its own capital to be able to issue credits. The Syrian government should keep majority control over the Reconstruction Bank. Beside this normal bank credit mechanism, a special "Hamiltonian credit" should be provided by the Government, either directly or through a National Bank, to the Reconstruction Bank. With this complementary credit mechanism, the government can administer enough credit for the fastest possible reconstruction of Syria.

When the government has given permission for a project to start, the Reconstruction Bank releases the necessary credit to an account for the project. The authorities or entrepreneur, who has the government contract for the reconstruction project, pays his suppliers and workers with the credit from this account. This will go on until the project is finished. All the new credits from the Reconstruction Bank then will have their security in the accomplishment of the finished projects.

How Can the Private Banks Be Mobilized for Reconstruction?

The right to issue credit is a crucial natural resource of a nation, to be used under the control of the government for the reconstruction. It is imperative that the credits are not recirculated into speculation or pyramid schemes, as in the banks of the Western globalized financial markets today. Therefore, the Syrian commercial banks have to be limited, and not be allowed to do any investment banking, like proprietary trading or the issuance of securities. This does not mean the banning of investment banking, but that part of each bank must be separated totally—regarding ownership, staffing, board officials, auditing, etc.—from any commercial banking.

From the time of U.S. President Franklin Roosevelt until 1999, there was a bank separation law in the United States called the Glass-Steagall Act, prescribing full bank separation. As long as that banking act was in force, there was no systemic crisis in the U.S. banking system. With such a bank separation law introduced in Syria, the commercial banking system can be mobilized for reconstruction. Only then will the credits from the Reconstruction Bank be recirculated in the banking system, creating ever-widening positive effects (like ripples in the water) in the physical economy.

Furthermore, as long as reconstruction goes on, the credits from private banks should be strictly controlled, to ensure that they are directed in accordance with the reconstruction plan to the categories of loans necessary for the physical needs of the industries and the people. The expansion of credit is thus tied to the physical economy.

With a regulated commercial banking system, the Reconstruction Bank can use the private banks to transmit its credits to the contracted entrepreneurs and to handle the payments. In such a case, the entrepreneur with a contract goes to his local bank, which in turn applies to the Reconstruction Bank for the credit allowed for the project.

Is the Nation Compelled To Get into Foreign Indebtedness To Reconstruct?

A domestic Hamiltonian credit system can enable all national labor and resources to be fully employed, but it cannot pay for what has to be imported. For that, foreign currency from export income, primarily, is needed, but this will not be enough for the reconstruction and development efforts. Syria will need huge loans in foreign currency to be able to import the necessary machines and equipment. These loans could be linked to the Reconstruction plan and the value of the projects they are to finance. In this way the loans and their interest rates can be adapted to the long-term repayment possibilities derived from the project.

Syria can not count on any bigger loans from the Western financial institutions in crisis. However, there is another method for getting credit in foreign currency even in the midst of a financial crisis: through bilateral trade agreements with interested Western nations. With this method, a nation can agree to issue a government credit in its own currency to finance export of machines or supplies to Syria. An array of such bilateral trade treaties with interested nations can provide the deliveries of the necessary foreign supplies for reconstruction.

The New Development bank of the BRICS nations has now been established to supply credit according to the new paradigm for a new just economic world order. The bank will provide credit according to the potential of projects in the future, and not from the current payment capacity of those nations initiating the project. The same principle will be applied by the many other new funds set up to enable the many New Silk Road projects. In this way an independent Syria has great potential to get its financing in foreign currency for important large-scale infrastructure projects.

As foreign indebtedness in the new paradigm corresponds to the new projects realized, it will be a good indebtedness. The more of such debt incurred to increase the potential of the nation, the better. Such debt will not be bondage, but a measurement of the amount Syria invests in its future potential.

What Syrian Potential Would Be Unleashed by a Credit System for Reconstruction?

1. The population as the carrier of all potential. Without priority being placed on food supplies, emergency housing, health care, education, and jobs, the potential of the whole population cannot be unleashed. For this, the broadest possible mobilization of the available resources of the nation is necessary, starting from government authorities all the way down to the micro level of local administrations. With a credit system available, in addition to their normal income, local administrations would be able to take part in the directed credits from the Reconstruction bank. This would put all available local resources into action to reconstruct schools, hospitals, power, and water systems, as well as food and other vital production that could be rapidly expanded.

Special credit lines can be directed to the former owners of industries and farms destroyed by the war, and also to entrepreneurs willing to start new businesses.

The targeting and destruction of all Syrian pharmaceutical industries by the enemy underscores its strategic importance and the same goes for the embattled oil, gas, and petrochemical sector. Also, the processing of the cotton production and other agricultural products in, for example, Syria's famous textile industry is a major reconstruction task, in addition to the whole industrial sector. Temporary work brigades mobilizing the unemployed could also be financed in the same way, to build what is necessary, and at the same time train the unemployed for more and more qualified work. The Army Corps of Engineers could provide the kernel for these work brigades, and with such reconstruction projects continue its defense of the Syrian people.

2. Reconstructing infrastructure and branches of industry with the most potential. With credits from

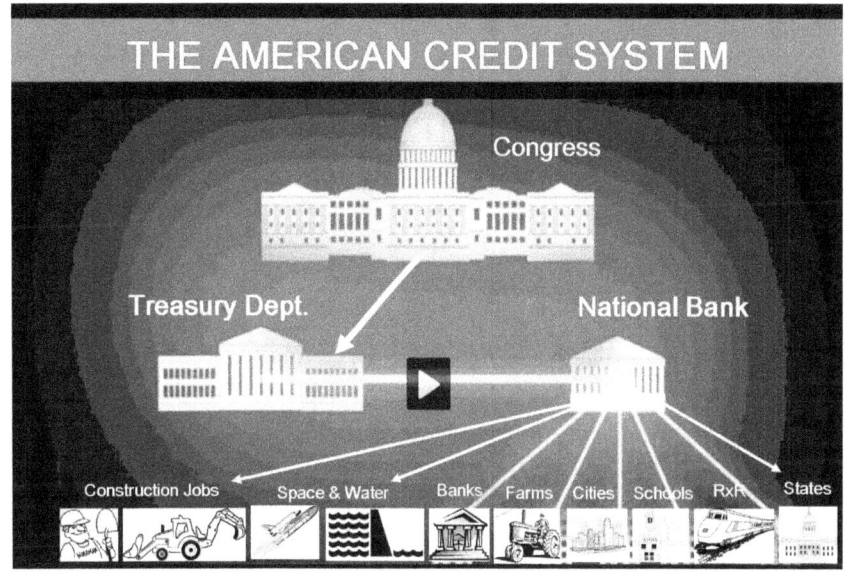

the Reconstruction Bank, Syria can finance its urgent infrastructure needs: energy, power, water, and communications. The credits can be expanded until all available qualified labor, materials, and machines in the nation are fully employed. In this way reconstruction can be organized in the most efficient way, according to the potential of future infrastructure development.

Thus also, the reconstruction can be oriented directly to the development of an infrastructure platform on the highest level of technology and productivity. Syria's war experience with the most advanced technologies for avionics, electronics, and machinery can be the basis for the introduction of new civilian branches of industry on such a new technological level, a kind of reconversion. A major upgrade of the chemical industry based on the strategic oil and gas resources can promote new industries producing fertilizers, plastics, iron, pharmaceuticals, and high tech products. Also, in the new paradigm of the BRICS, the nuclear industry that was destroyed by Israel can be resurrected both for power production and water desalination, and bring Syria into the era of isotope exploration.

3. The potential of new technology in the reconstruction. Special attention and credit should be directed to finding possibilities for jumps in technological evolution, since old equipment has to be replaced anyway. For instance, new power cables could be paired with telecommunication fibre-optic cables The criteria for what technology should be prioritized is its energy density. Just as the increase of energy density in the weapon of the soldier, considering precision and power per square inch, increases the impact on the enemy,

FIGURE 2
Mediterranean Basin Great Infrastructure Projects

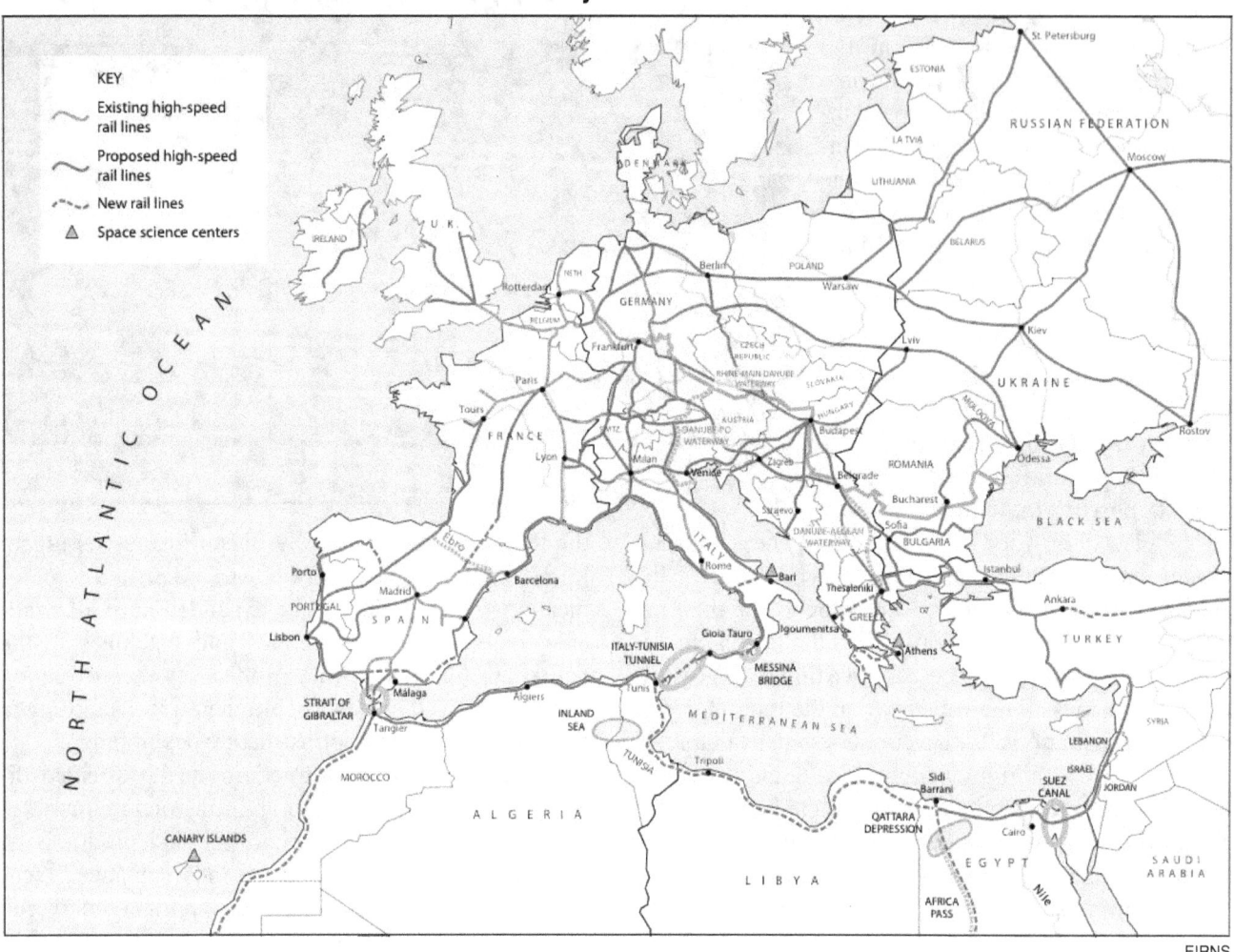

An overview of the projects profiled in EIR's *"Program for an Economic Miracle in Southern Europe, the Mediterranean Region, and Africa." The full report can be accessed at www.larouchepub.com.*

energy density is the parameter for the peaceful worker to increase his productivity and to find the highest potential for profitability in the physical economy.

4. Projection of the potential of the New Silk Road into Syria. The potential for connecting Syria with infrastructure routes from the Mediterranean Sea, the Indian Ocean, the Red Sea, the Caspian Sea, and the Black Sea has been the visionary idea of President Bashar Assad in his "Five Seas Strategy." The massive growth of the BRICS countries and all their initiatives to develop the New Silk Road strategy, both on land and on sea, will be projected into Syria, as long as this vision is guiding Syria's planning for new infrastructure.

The Silk Road strategy is not about just transport, but how two international development corridors, one East-West and the other North-South, will bring long-

term vitality and growth to the ancient crossroads of Syria. Besides railways, it includes a broad range of other infrastructure, such as pipelines, water projects, industrial zones, agriculture. as well as city building. The New Silk Road paradigm puts on the planning table such visions as the greening of the desert, diminishing the effects of sand storms, and reconquering of vast desert territories for agriculture and settlement in cooperation with neighboring nations, for a maximum use and development of the water resources.

How Can the New Silk Road Be Projected Into Syria?

1. The link to Baghdad and Teheran. The strategy of China's "One Belt, One Road" to develop the old Silk road into development corridors with modern transport systems and infrastructure, is reaching into Europe, but also into Southwest Asia, Egypt, and Africa. A land route with a railway will be built via Iran to Egypt along the route from Teheran over Kermanshah to Baghdad, Amman, and Aqaba. Through a planned tunnel at Sharm el Sheik, the railway will reach Egypt and its capital Cairo. This new railway will come close to Syria and enable a railway to be built from the Syrian end station of the railway along the Euphrates river, Deir Ezzor, to Baghdad.

In this way, the old Silk Road along the Euphrates from Basra will have a railway connection and become the main East-West development corridor for Syria; it will bring new energy to the devastated industrial zones of Raqqa and Aleppo. Such a railway, built in cooperation with Iraq, will be a big step toward making the Five Seas Strategy a reality, as it connects Syria to the Arabian Gulf and the Indian Ocean.

The railway connection from Baghdad and Teheran would also bring trade on the overland Silk routes from China and India. The main Middle Silk Road corridor through Western China and Central Asia passes through Teheran. The land route from India is also within reach, as the Iranian railway network is built all the way to Zahedan on the border to Pakistan, which has a rail connection from India that will be opened sometime in the near future.

The railway from Teheran enables also the connection from the Caspian Sea Region, as the next step in the "Five Seas Strategy." The transports from Russia on the so-called North-South Corridor linking up St. Petersburg with the Iranian harbor Bandar Abbas, and later also Chabahar, on the Indian Ocean coast, will go both on the Caspian Sea and on railways on both sides, which also will become connections for Syria.

Basra is within reach to be connected to the planned high speed railway along the Western side of the Arabian Gulf from UAE to Kuwait. This railway will eventually be linked up to Oman and Yemen. All these trade routes will, like the old Silk Road, be projected into Syria towards Aleppo. Then this development corridor will continue to the devastated Idlib region, and then down to the port of Latakia, which will have to be expanded.

A next step to open up the old East-West Silk Road routes will be to build the railway from Deir Ezzor to Tadmor/Palmyra, the legendary Silk Road city, where Silk Road festivals were held each year before the war. This missing link will create a railway from

Teheran and Baghdad directly to Damascus and Beirut.

2. The link to Cairo. The dynamic development of Egypt, with the giant planned industrial zones along the New Suez Canal, will be brought directly into Syria when the railway link from Cairo to Amman in Jordan will be opened. The old railway from Jordan can be reconstructed as a high-speed railway to Damascus, and to the big cities Homs and Hama all the way up to Aleppo in the North. In this way also the Red Sea Region will acquire its railway link to Syria from the Aqaba harbor. The Egyptian plans for rail connections along the Nile river to the South, will not only bring trade to Syria from Sudan, but also along a planned railway from Eastern Africa through Ethiopia, the fastest growing economy in the world.

When the Hedjaz railway has been rebuilt as a high-speed system, Damascus again will become a main point of departure for journeys to Medina and Mecca. A connection from Yemen will also be opened along this route, and also one from Africa through the planned tunnel under the Bab El Mandeb strait from Djibouti.

From Egypt the construction of the stalled Arabic Gas Pipe Line will resume, so it can be connected in the Homs region in Syria to the new planned gas pipeline from Iran to Syria. This pipeline will greatly facilitate the export of gas production, and the distribution of the production needed for domestic consumption for all the nations involved.

3. The Northern link from Europe, the Black Sea Region, and Russia. When the Northern border of Syria has been opened, the main transport route across Syria will be opened with the railway from Europe, which will soon become a high-speed rail connection to Cairo. This will bring energy to all Syria's major war-torn cities: Aleppo, Hama, Homs and Damascus. In each city, a local transport system could be speedily built, if the low noise maglev technology is chosen. This technology has a higher speed and energy density than others. At the same time it can be built rapidly because the guideways are placed on pillars, and thus avoid creating problems with work on archeological sites such as halted the construction of the subway system in Damascus in the past. The railway, the local transport systems, and other infrastructure will integrate the cities and their regions into a broad North-South development corridor right through the whole Western part of Syria.

In addition, the Chinese trade with Europe along the main Middle Silk Road corridor through Iran and Turkey will be connected in Turkey to the North-South development corridor through Syria. Through Turkey, trade will be drawn from Armenia and Azerbaijan and through them also from Russia. The Black Sea region will be connected into Syria through the Samsun and Istanbul ports, the latter of which is also the destination for the new "Viking Rail Line" from the Klaipeda port in Lithuania and will create a trade route from the Baltic Sea Region and Sweden.

4. The Mediterranean link. After the inauguration of the New Suez Canal in August of this year, enormous ships can now bring new cargo flows from China and India on the Maritime Silk Road into the Mediterranean Sea. There are on-going construction and plans for expansion of a series of ports such as Piraeus in Greece and Taranto, Crotone, and Gioia Tauro in Southern Italy, to handle these new cargo flows and to build high-speed rail lines, northwards, to Central Europe through both Italy and the Balkans. China is participating in the planning of a new canal through the Balkans, from Thessaloniki along the rivers Axios/Vardar and Drina, all the way up to the European main artery of transport, the Donau river, which draws traffic from the great Rhine river in Germany. This will also enable transport to Syria, if Syria's main Mediterranean ports Tartous and Latakia are expanded.

The whole Mediterranean Sea should become a region of development to counter the economic crisis and unemployment in Northern Africa and Southern Europe. To make this happen an *EIR* task force put together a Marshall plan for the region: Program for an Economic Miracle in Southern Europe, The Mediterranean region, and Africa, with many of the projects of the future listed, such as tunnels between Sicily and Tunisia, and under the Straits of Gibraltar.

Along the North African coast, Egypt will construct its nuclear station for power and for desalination of sea water, which will enable development of agriculture, industry, and settlements. Desalination projects are possible on other places along the coast of Africa, but are especially necessary at the Gaza Strip, which is running out of fresh water. Tunisia has a great potential in the salty marshes called Sud. Since early in the Twentieth Century, there have been plans for water projects there, to remove the salt and make a vast region in the south of Tunisia and eastern Algeria into a fruitful agriculture area.

Other important projects on the table are designed to direct water from Central Africa to the north. The Africa Pass project plans to bring the water all the way to western Egypt close to Libya. There the great Qattara Depression, which is under the sea level of the Mediterranean, should be filled up with fresh water, forming a big lake. In addition to new railways and roads along the canal through the Sahara to a big port on the Mediterranean Sea, an array of cities can be built and a vast desert region can be populated.

This is also the intention with the Transaqua project to bring surplus water from the Congo River in a canal into the Lake Chad basin. This brings enormous development opportunities by saving the Chad lake and the opening of a vast region, in the southern Sahara, for resettlement and development. The New Development Bank of the BRICS nations could make these projects possible.

It is necessary to pull Europe and the United States into cooperation with the BRICS-nations around this development policy. In this way the Western nations would begin the process of developing their own real economic potentials, instead their continued collapse with their sick financial system and their genocidal war policy.

For further study
In English: Details about the Hamiltonian credit system:

Draft Legislation: To Restore the Original Bank of the United States. Click here.

General history about the Hamiltonian credit system:

https://larouchepac.com/credit-system

The recovery accomplished with the Hamiltonian credit system by U.S. President Franklin Roosevelt's New Deal:

http://www.larouchepub.com/eiw/public/2002/eirv29n34-20020906/eirv29n34-20020906_056-fdrs_reconstruction_finance_corp.pdf

and

http://www.larouchepub.com/eiw/public/2006/2006_20-29/2006-21/pdf/26-30_621_ecoarmycorps.pdf

and

http://www.larouchepub.com/eiw/public/2006/2006_10-19/2006-11/pdf/48-59_611_eco.pdf

In Arabic

http://arabic.larouchepub.com/2015/10/24/752/

In German

http://www.solidaritaet.com/neuesol/2015/44/phoenix.htm

In Swedish

http://www.larouche.se/node/4134

FIGURE 3
Eurasian Rail Network Plan as First Presented by LaRouche's Associates in 1992

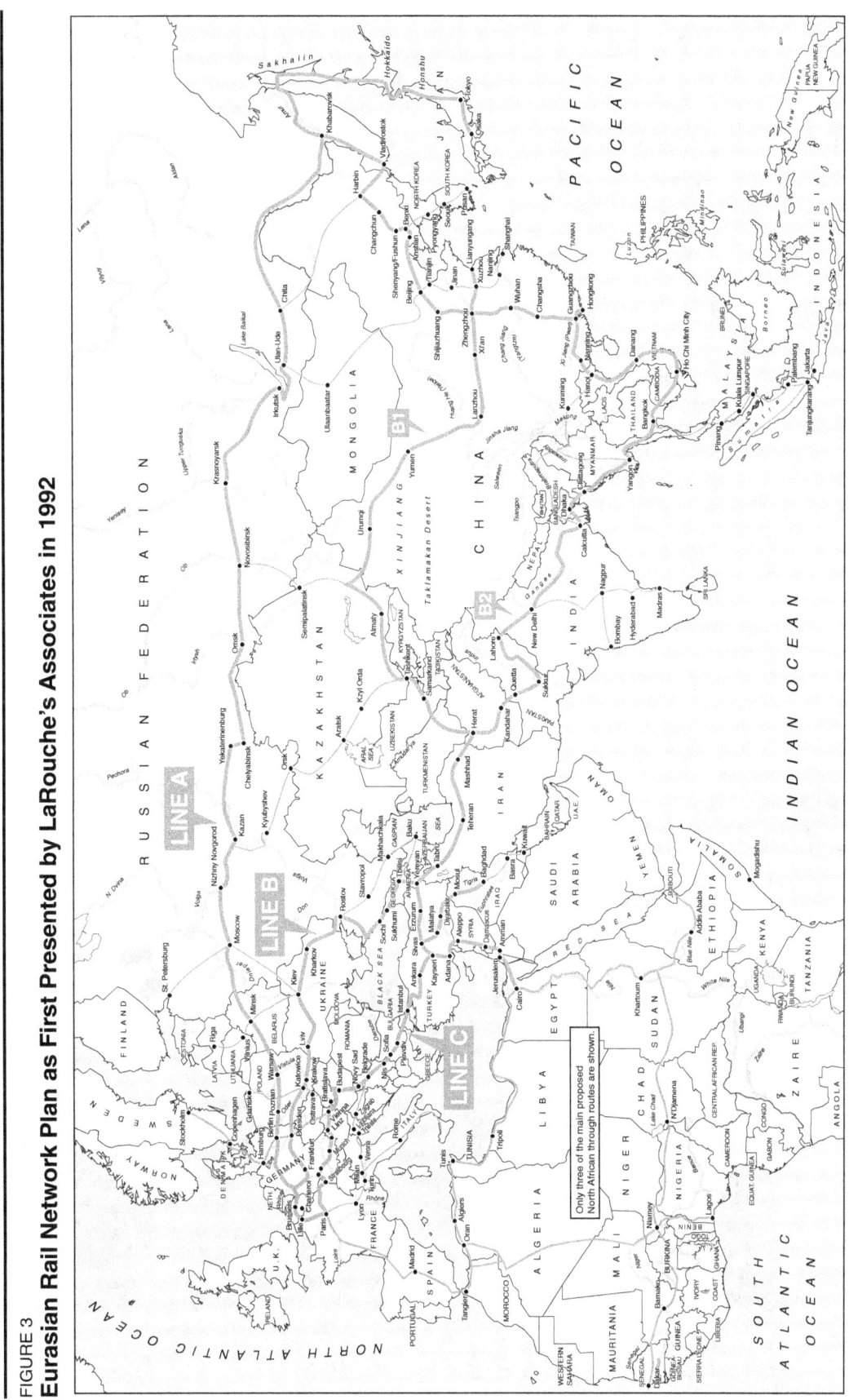

President Assad's 'Five Seas Vision'

Syrian President Bashar Assad launched his "Five Seas Vision" officially in 2004, a vision aimed at taking advantage of Syria's geographic position to put it at the center of a regional energy and transportation network. Before the foreign-orchestrated war on Syria began in 2011, President Assad criss-crossed the region with large delegations, visiting neighboring countries and beyond to pursue his plan. Many agreements were made, including with Turkey, Romania, Ukraine, Azerbaijan, Iran, Iraq, and Lebanon.

These agreements included the following huge pipeline projects: a gas pipeline from Iran; a pipeline into Turkey linking up in with the planned Nabucco gas pipeline from Azerbaijan; and the rebuilding of the oil pipeline from Northern Iraq into Syria. Syria's official five-year plan, launched in 2004, projected vigorous measures for building the roads, ports, and pipelines inside the country necessary for realizing the "Five Seas Vision."

President Assad's vision, however, goes beyond the region. Speaking to *The Weekly Middle East Reporter* Aug. 1, 2009 Assad explained his idea: "Once the economic space between Syria, Turkey, Iraq and Iran becomes integrated, we would link the Mediterranean, Caspian, Black Sea, and the [Persian] Gulf ... we aren't just important in the Middle East... Once we link these four seas, we become the unavoidable intersection of the whole world in investment, transport, and more."

With this policy, President Assad was acting in the same spirit that launched a sea change of independent South-South relations in the wake of the 2003 British/U.S.-led invasion of Iraq. The worldwide protests and resistance to that war formed itself into an international revolt against the global world order, leading up to the formation of the BRICS Alliance. As Dania

courtesy of Ulf Sandmark

Co-author Ulf Sandmark (center) and Swedish architect Greger Ahlberg (left) with other members of the delegation of the Swedish association the Syrian Support Committee for Democracy, and the head of the Umayyad Mosque in Damascus (second from left), during their November 2014 visit to Syria.

Akkad described it in *Syria Times* in 2011, the "Five Seas Vision" "should be taken as a symbol that Syria will no longer depend on the Unitee States and its main allies for stability, a message that many other countries—Venezuela, Brazil and Argentina, for example—have also been asserting in recent years." (See article)

The Jamestown Foundation's Christina Lin brings up the obvious historic background to the "Five Seas Vision" in her article "The Caspian Sea: China's Silk Road Strategy Converges with Damascus," published Aug. 19, 2010:

> Such a policy, which now carries Assad's signature, is not new. It existed during the heyday of the Umayyad Dynasty (661-750), when it was actually six rather than five seas, reaching as far as the Baltic Sea where the Umayyads—the first great Muslim dynasty to rule the Empire of the Caliphate—excelled as merchants, rather than as politicians or military conquerors.

That empire covered more than five million square miles, around one trillion hectares, reaching far and wide with trade routes and political influence felt throughout India, China, North Africa, and Spain. Damascus, the legitimate child and former capital of that empire, sees it as very possible to re-connect the six seas in today's world. This policy envisions a network of operations all running through Syria for the transfer of oil and gas, goods, manpower, and ideas, connecting the Caucasus in the north with the Arab Gulf in the south, Iran in the east, and Europe in the west. ... Collectively, if these countries are linked via Syria, they add up to a human cluster of no less than 288 million people—a bloc that cannot be ignored, and perhaps not defeated.

The perspective of the formation of such a bloc is more than enough to explain why the geopoliticians of the West today insist that Assad must go.

—Ulf Sandmark

There Is Life After the Euro!

Program for an Economic Miracle in Southern Europe, the Mediterranean Region, and Africa

AN **EIR** SPECIAL REPORT

CONTENTS

Introduction by Helga Zepp-LaRouche
Greece, and a Marshall Plan for the Mediterranean Basin
Spain: Bridge to African Development
The Rebirth of Italy's Mezzogiorno

Africa Pass
The Transaqua Project
North Africa: The Blue Revolution
What Europe Can Learn from Argentina
A German Economic Miracle for Europe

http://www.larouchepub.com/special_report/2012/spec_rpt_program_medit.pdf

The Galaxy Project: An Introduction

by Benjamin Deniston

This is an edited transcript of the first of several classes on the Galaxy Project of the LaRouche PAC Basement Team. The video is available on the LaRouche PAC website as the Weekly Report of the New Paradigm for Mankind Program for Wednesday, Oct. 28, 2015.

I'm glad to be here today in front of a live audience in a new format for our New Paradigm Show on the LaRouche PAC website. This is the beginning of a class series on what we've called the Galaxy Project, or the Galactic Science Driver Program. This is an introductory class; there will probably be five to eight classes, delving into aspects of this Galaxy Project that the LaRouche PAC Basement Team has tackled as a new program.

Given the nature of this event, it might be useful to restate very briefly, re-situate—I'm a part of the LaRouche PAC Science Team, or as Mr. LaRouche has named us, the Basement Team. It's a scientific program, part of a scientific research team, rooted in attempting to revive, re-develop, and carry forward a very specific current of physical science rooted in the Renaissance. You can go back farther, but much of our focussed work has been rooted in the Classical Golden Renaissance in Italy—the development of modern science centered around the work of Nicholas of Cusa and his followers through Johannes Kepler, and on through followers of this specific school of scientific thought, which has been largely lost in the recent century.

What we've taken on here is the prospect of looking at the Galactic System as a next stage in the scientific frontiers for mankind, continuing in this specific tradition of real physical science. It's about the way people approach scientific questions, but it's also about what mankind is. What is mankind's nature and role in the Universe? That was very clearly understood in the Renaissance. There was a very clear, unified concept underlying the development of science, and it's been lost in science today. So when we look at this question of

mankind going to the Galaxy as a new level of science, we're also talking about a new level for mankind, a new stage for mankind as a species.

Mr. LaRouche has defined the Galactic level as a frontier project. He has pointed to Johannes Kepler as a critical reference point, as Kepler had demonstrated the validity of this Renaissance conception of man—and carried forward the founding of modern science—in his discovery of the Solar System as a single organized system, accessible uniquely to the mind of man, as Kepler was able to demonstrate.

In that same tradition, today we look to the Galaxy as the next frontier for mankind. We're looking at the prospect of mankind becoming a galactic species. I say that just in honor, or rather in dishonor, of the new Star Wars movie,—most people have seen the advertisements of the latest episode in the Star Wars sci-fi saga that's coming out this winter. This is a good opportunity to emphasize—when we say mankind can become a Galactic species—we're not talking about the pop-science, sci-fi conception of jumping in your spaceship and hopping around to different parts of the Galaxy, and we're a Galactic species when we travel through the Galaxy.

That's not what we're talking about. We're talking about something much more profound in the way mankind, you could say, enters the Galaxy, or becomes a Galactic species. It is not a question of where we physically place people, or place objects. It's a question of where mankind is, in a uniquely human, mentally creative way, with respect to the nature of organization of the Universe. That's what we're talking about.

How is it that mankind can come into being in the Universe from the standpoint of certain higher-order processes, in a way that no animal species ever could, and understand that that really is a sacred process? We're re-defining our understanding of the Universe through revolutionary breakthroughs, some of which we will discuss today; but we're also re-defining our

ESO, Creative Commons

Humankind, the galactic species, observes our own galaxy. The Milky Way, a bright band of stars partly obscured by galactic clouds of gas and dust, is what we can see of the Home Galaxy with the naked eye. Because we reside in the galactic plane, we have an edge-on view. The laser beam is pointing to the galactic center. The many stars distributed across the sky are also in the galactic plane; because they are foreground objects, they appear not to be. This is the Very Large Telescope in northern Chile, operated by the European Southern Observatory.

existence in the Universe at the same time.

That's going to be the concluding point of the introduction today. The guiding theme throughout this series is that we're not just talking about finding some new law that describes some aspect of the Galaxy; we're talking about how we raise mankind to a fundamentally new level of existence in the Universe from the standpoint of a Galactic Principle, a Galactic level of existence for mankind, as I would put it.

Climate and Water

You may be familiar with the LaRouche PAC activity with respect to the issue of water and drought if you are following our website. We've discussed the issue of water from the Galactic standpoint. I think it's very useful as an opening example, just to get thinking in the proper framework, the proper conception.

There's much talk of a water crisis going on in California, the West Coast of the United States, and other parts of the world. There's a lot of discussion about the lack of sufficient water to sustain human activity. As we've shown in some of our work, it's a pretty ridiculous claim. There's plenty of water out there, but there are Malthusian fools like California Governor Jerry

Brown, who just don't want the water supply, because they don't want population growth. They don't want the level of population they have.

Aside from that genocidal ideology, there's a real lack of understanding of what mankind could be doing to develop the resources we need. With water supply in particular, there are a lot of options. There's desalination, and there are ways to redirect water from one place to another. Those are options.

But as we've discussed and presented on the LaRouche PAC website, there is also another avenue that actually takes us to a higher perspective, which is understanding how our Solar System is actually a subsumed component of our larger Galactic System, and that the water cycle, as we currently depend upon it, the water cycle as it exists on the Earth, is heavily influenced and controlled by effects from our Galaxy; specifically, the atmospheric flows of water vapor throughout the world, how water vapor behaves in the atmosphere, and the conditions that cause it to fall as rain, are largely influenced and controlled by radiation effects from our Galaxy, by what is called cosmic radiation.

We've been learning in recent decades that cosmic ray flux is actually a critical factor in determining how water behaves, and also how climate behaves. We'll get into some of this a bit later; this is a new insight into how radiation effects—energetic effects, not coming from our Earth, our Sun, or our Solar System, but coming from the subsuming environment of our Galaxy—play an active, day-to-day role in affecting something as simple and seemingly Earth-centered as water, your local water supply.

What does that mean for mankind? It means that we have a potential to control these processes and influence the water cycle in a completely new way. I would direct people to the work we have already done on this, on technologies being developed, and technologies that have been demonstrated and are in use, that can be used to manage atmospheric water flows, by tapping into the

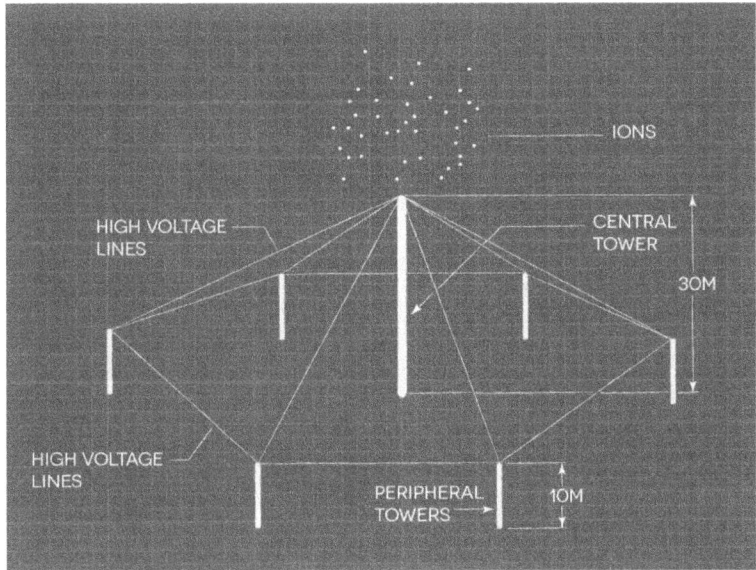

Tapping the Galaxy for water: This is a schematic of the concept behind the project undertaken by Russian scientist Sergey Pulinets in northern Mexico, where ionization towers were used to stimulate rain in arid regions.

same types of processes that we get from our Galactic System that affect atmospheric water vapor.

So, that is one example of the type of thing we're talking about, as we gain a greater understanding of the fact that mankind doesn't just live on some isolated planet by ourselves, not even in an isolated Solar System, but that the activity on our planet, in our Solar System, is intimately connected to, and related to, these larger-scale Galactic processes, the larger-scale Galactic System, which contains us. And water is an example. When we develop these higher insights, as mankind, that gives us a greater capability to act, a greater capability to increase our potential as a species on this planet.

That's an example of the integral connection between mankind's scientific understanding of the Universe and mankind's ability to change the nature of his existence, even on Earth, but from the standpoint of these higher-order principles, these higher-order processes, which we can discover and then act upon. It's just one example of some of the work that's actually led to this Galaxy Project, this science-driver program.

But beyond this or some other examples, the project goes to some very fundamental areas of science. Today I want to focus primarily on the method of approach going into this whole project. In preparing for today's presentation, a series of discussions we had with Mr. LaRouche in the summer of 2014 came to mind.

Vernadsky and the Biosphere

We were talking about the role of Vladimir Vernadsky, the leading Russian scientist, contemporary of Einstein—the role of Vernadsky, situated in the longer arc of the development of modern science. Mr. LaRouche defined what he called his triad conception of the development of science. He said, if we want to look at where we need to go with science today, look at the initiation of modern science through the work of Cusa (1401-1464) and Filippo Brunelleschi (1377-1446), and then carried through with the work of Kepler (1571-1630). With this triad of scientific thinkers, you define the initiation of modern science. And he defined a concluding "bookend" triad of recent scientific thinkers that exemplifies the farthest we've gone in the development of scientific thought: namely, Max Planck (1858-1947), Albert Einstein (1879-1955), and Vladimir Vernadsky (1863-1945).

We talked about looking at the development of modern science, book-ended by these two triads of thinkers. I thought his reference to the role of Vernadsky in that development was useful for the current project. I want to highlight one passage about Vernadsky from that discussion with Mr. LaRouche and then see how it plays into the current Galaxy Project. Mr. LaRouche said:

> You have to look at Vernadsky in parallel with the previous triad. Kepler discovered the Solar System, but the Solar System was not the concept of systems. Kepler had solved a problem, but he does not solve *the* problem. The idea of the Solar System was not a concept of systems, and what you get with Vernadsky is the systems. We don't get systems as such, with Vernadsky, but we get the implications of the systems. In other words, you can project from Vernadsky—you can go to the idea of a general principle of systems.
>
> And that is what I wanted to concentrate on. In other words, it seems on first pass—you say, "Oh, how nice, Vernadsky has produced something which fits everything that is required for a new system." But you say, "Wait a minute; this is not just a new system, it is a model for systems." This is the standard you use for trying to

Modern science was founded by this triad of scientific thinkers from the Fourteenth to Seventeenth Centuries: from left to right, Italian architect Filippo Brunelleschi, Cardinal Nicholas of Cusa, and Johannes Kepler.

find new evidence which will tell you what the key is for the higher order systems.

I thought this was a provocative conception that Lyn had put forward. Coming from that quote in particular, and from some of the context of our discussions with him at the time, was his idea of looking at the Universe, the larger astronomical processes, as a nesting of successively higher ordered systems, and the question of what we can take from Vernadsky's approach; where Vernadsky had taken scientific thought, scientific investigations, as a more generalized investigation of systems of processes; and how we can use that insight in approaching some of the new questions about the Solar System and the relation of the Solar System to the Galactic System.

We were discussing with Mr. LaRouche the concept of the Earth being a subsumed part of the Solar System as a whole, and the Solar System being nested within the larger process of the Galaxy as a system. And then— going to an even higher order—super-galactic structures on a scale of maybe tens of galaxies to even much larger scales, and looking for principles of organization and development, even on these much larger scales.

What I took from this quote and our discussions with Mr. LaRouche, and my understanding of Vernadsky's work, was the ability to begin to look at systems generally in a non-reductionist fashion. Vernadsky did this in a clear initial way in his work on the biosphere, and that is what he's most famous for, as the originator of the conception of the biosphere. He was fascinated with the distinction between life and non-life. He was fascinated with a lot of things. He was an amazing thinker. He covered an immense area of different fields, different sciences, including fields he created.

Especially towards the end of his life, Vernadsky was fascinated with the qualitative, infinite distinction of life from non-life, and how you understand and demonstrate that, and thereby better understand life. And he came very clearly to his conception of the biosphere— his idea that you can't *just* study individual organisms themselves. That can be done. You can find some useful things in doing it. But if you want to get at the principle of how life is expressed on the planet Earth, the distinction of life from non-life as expressed on Earth, you have to go beyond individual organisms.

He had famously said, you can't abstract an organism from the biosphere as a whole. It doesn't exist in isolation. It exists as a component, a part, of the biosphere that sustains it—that it contributes to, and that in turn sustains it. In the opening pages of his book, *The Biosphere,* his seminal work on this subject, he explicitly defines what we would call a non-reductionist approach to the biosphere, saying we're going to investigate the biospheric system as a whole as a single harmonious process, a single harmonious mecha-

The most advanced level of scientific thinking to date has come from what LaRouche has identified as a second triad of scientists from the late Nineteenth into the Twentieth Century: from left to right, Max Planck, Vladimir Vernadsky, and Albert Einstein.

nism—these are the terms he uses—without assuming that we can just explain it away on the basis of the component interactions in the small.

'Biogenic Migration of Atoms'

What I see Mr. LaRouche referring to in Vernadsky, is a breakthrough demonstration of how to study a larger organized system, as a system, as a single process, and not just a collection of parts—studying it from the anti-entropic standpoint. We get a very interesting perspective for the investigation of the Galaxy, these larger-scale systems, when you look at Vernadsky's scientific insights into evolution, into the development of the biosphere, in particular, what Vernadsky defines as his Second Biogeochemical Principle. He says:

This Biogeochemical Principle, which I will call the Second Biogeochemical Principle, can be formulated thus: The evolution of species, leading to the creation of new, stable, living forms, must move in the direction of an increasing of the biogenic migration of atoms in the biosphere.

And he goes on to say:

This Second Biogeochemical Principle indicates, in my opinion, with an infallible logic, the existence of a determined direction in the sense of how the processes of evolution must take place.

Now this was in the mid-1920s. Studies of the fossil record were relatively young at the time, and we certainly have a much better understanding of the evolution of different forms of life now, nearly a century later. But even at this early time, Vernadsky was able to develop this clear insight into not just the biosphere as a process at any one time, but what are certain governing characteristics of how the biosphere has developed over time as a system. A key concept that he developed for investigating life, the activity of life on the planet, is what he calls the biogenic migration of atoms. That is, how biological processes, living processes, incorporate and move the chemical elements around the surface of the Earth. This is a metric of how living processes, living organisms, reshape and reorganize the medium of the surface of the Earth, creating the biosphere, creating forms of life.

Vernadsky often spoke in these terms, and examined the biosphere as a state of organization of the geochemical medium, the Earth's crust. He would investigate this from the standpoint of how much life, living organisms, is transforming, acting on, the surface of the planet. And his insight into evolution, the development of life, the development of the biosphere over time, is that this process must increase. That is how evolution must necessarily take place, he says, and it is intimately tied to, and governed by, the increase in the rate of activity of life.

This has been confirmed in a number of ways in more recent studies now, nearly a century later, and we see very clearly various indications that this is the principle of evolution. This is the principle of the development of life, the increasing rate of activity, the increas-

FIGURE 1

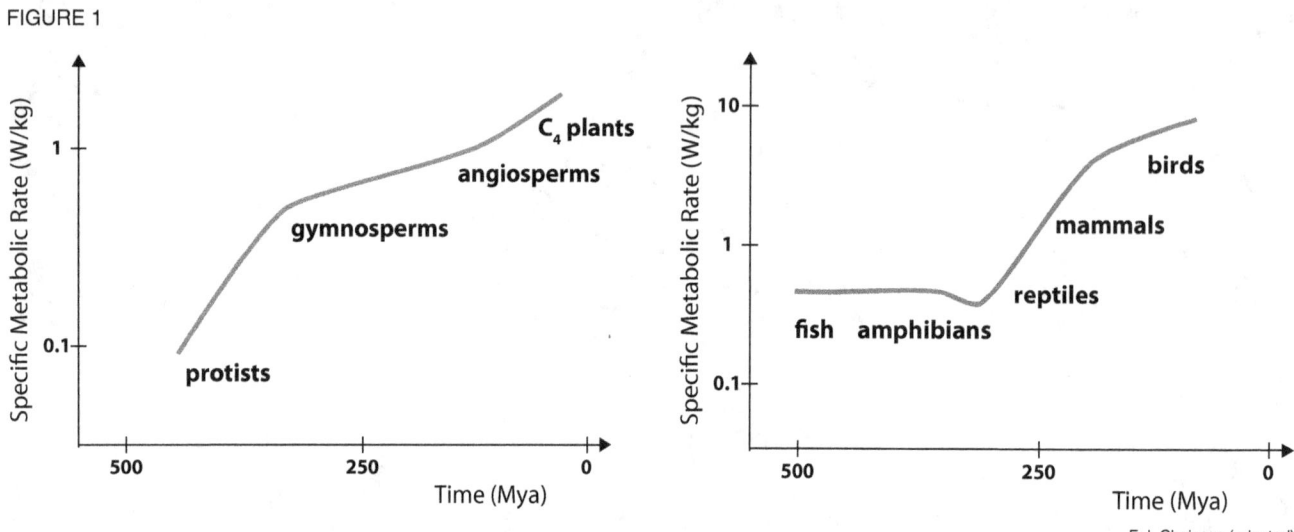

E.J. Chaisson (adapted)

From these charts, showing the increase of the rate of energy flow per kilogram of body mass, for both photosynthesizers and animals, one can very clearly see the evolutionary direction of life, toward increased energy-flux density. In the diagram, metabolic rate is expressed as watts per kilogram. The time scale is expressed in millions of years ago.

ing biogenic migration of atoms. We see that species now living have replaced earlier species, and that new types of life have emerged with characteristically higher rates of activity, higher rates of biogenic migration of atoms than earlier forms of life. A lot of the more recent work is completely consistent with the thesis that Vernadsky developed earlier.

Energy-Flux Density

We could introduce another term, energy-flux density, a conception that Mr. LaRouche developed in his study of another type of system, another process, human economic processes. Energy-flux density is the energy flow through a surface or a volume, the density or the rate of the flow of energy, the transformation of energy. It has an intimate connection to Vernadsky's idea of the biogenic migration of atoms. They're very closely connected ideas. In some of the work we've done in the Basement, you can see very clearly the evolutionary direction of life, and you can study it with these metrics. You're really looking at evolution of life being governed and driven by this process of increasing energy-flux density. (**Figure 1**)

Those are a few elements providing insight into the characteristics that we can derive and define from the earlier Vernadskyan anti-reductionist approach to the conception of systems. Perhaps what we want to define a bit more precisely is, how do we study anti-entropic developing processes? Vernadsky had laid an initial groundwork for studying the development of the bio-sphere as a characteristic anti-entropic developing process.

We see a very similar thing if we look at another type of process involving another principle, human economic activity. I will come back to that later. But Vernadsky's work—his work on the biosphere, the work he started to do on evolution, and the work he began on the study of human life as distinct from animal life—led to what he defined as the Noösphere, the domain of human activity directed by human thought; it's a very similar thing. You have an investigation of a larger scale process of organization and development, which you want to understand as a whole, and discover its characteristics. What can we define as the internal metrics which tell you about that thing as a system, without assuming we can just explain it away by reductionist methods? This is where Mr. LaRouche's work really comes in on a higher level—studying human economic processes.

Coming back to the quote from Mr. LaRouche, his emphasis on the importance of Vernadsky's work provides an important and unique perspective for orienting the Galactic Science Driver Program. And as we discussed with Mr. LaRouche at the time, one thing we want to look at is how to apply this framework of thought, this Vernadsky-LaRouche approach to defining, studying, and understanding the development of anti-entropic systems. We want to take that as a basis for thinking about generalizing to the larger-scale astronomical processes. That was part of the discussion with Mr. LaRouche that I quoted from.

FIGURE 2

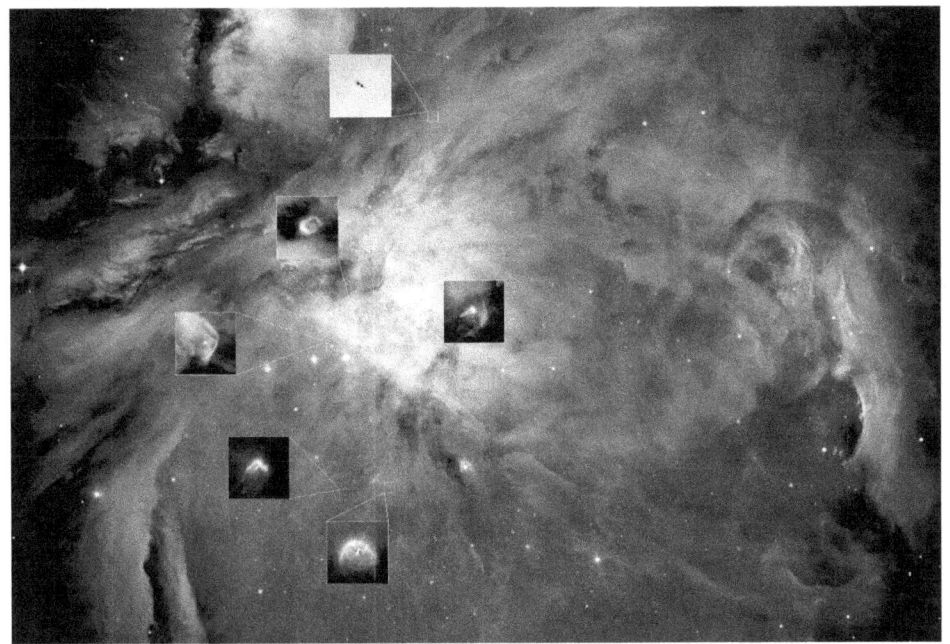

ESA/NASA Hubble

A giant molecular cloud, with a few regions blown up to show the kind of detail not visible at this scale. Our Galaxy has many such clouds. Spectroscopic analysis of the light received from such clouds shows a predominance of molecular hydrogen (H_2) and carbon monoxide (CO). But there are also much more complex molecules, including organic compounds such as CH_3OH, C_2H_5OH, and CH_3OCH_3.

Solar System as a Process

Now today we are looking at the existence of the Earth within the Solar System as a process, and the Solar System within the Galaxy. But what are these things? People just think of a collection of objects. The Solar System—you get the picture in your textbook. The big ball of the Sun and the planets with their orbits drawn in. You get this sense-perceptual picture of it, this set of bodies, but what is the process underlying that? What is it as a process of change? What is it as a process of development?

I think there's a lot to pull from the method used by Vernadsky and Lyn in studying life, in studying human economic processes, to start to look at other aspects of these higher order systems from a similar standpoint. Don't just see it as a collection of objects. Where did it come from? Where is it going? What are the governing characteristics of it as a process of change, as a process of development? How is it then situated within the next higher order system? You won't apply it in the exact same way, but in general, we could approach the idea of what is our Solar System in this way.

To the best of our knowledge, our Solar System came from something like this giant molecular cloud (**Figure 2**). We always thank NASA for the nice images. A giant molecular cloud—very exciting descriptive name, I know. Giant, it's big. Molecular, it's got a bunch of molecules in it. It's like a cloud. But the Galaxy is filled with them. In our Galaxy and other galaxies, you get these giant cloud structures of gas and dust. And in these you can see what—as far as our present knowledge tells us—are the initial processes of new stars forming, of new stellar systems, with new planetary systems around new stars.

Hopefully, the United States can get its financing act together and finally put up the James Webb Space Telescope as the successor to the Hubble; then we'll be getting some even nicer images of these things. But we can actually peer into the very early stages of something pretty remarkable: some large, relatively homogeneous, relatively unstructured clouds of gas and dust, mostly hydrogen, some helium, and then a sprinkling of other stuff, as the raw material for forming something like a solar system, highly organized, highly differentiated, highly structured, going from a fundamentally lower state of organization, to a much higher state of organization. New types of physical chemistry, new types of processes, are occurring. You have the potential to get a much greater dimension of physical chemistry, of types of minerals, types of molecular structures.

You even get the development of the array of elements of the periodic table out of these processes through nucleosynthesis. To our present knowledge, the array of elements comes from the processes associated with the development and life cycle of stars. I would argue that it is an anti-entropic process. Stellar nucleosynthesis is the idea that the heavy elements have been produced by nuclear fusion reactions occurring in stars, beginning initially with mostly hydrogen, some helium, and maybe a little bit of lithium, and then developing the whole array out of that through fusion processes.

There are also some interesting studies indicating that even the life cycle of a single star—again, assuming we have a decent understanding of the life cycle of a star—is characterized by increasing energy-flux density (**Figure 3**). You are measuring the energy of the star per unit of time per unit of mass as it changes during the star's evolutionary changes (shown in giga-years, Gy). As stars go through the life cycle, their energy-flux density increases while they are building us a nice periodic table out of some basic raw materials.

A New Era of Science

This, then, is the direction that I think we want to go in, in continuing a LaRouche-Vernadsky approach to studying these larger-scale systems to lead to a new era of science. In modern science today, these phenomena are all just explained away as a consequence of a certain set of fixed laws, a certain fixed set of properties of interactions. But what is completely ignored is the approach that Vernadsky took in studying the biosphere. What is the system as a whole? What is it doing? Where does it come from? Where is it going? Without assuming that we can reduce everything to its parts, what is this thing as a process of development of change? And how do we begin to think about it from that standpoint? And how do we understand what is the principle governing it? And where do we go from here?

We are part of this Solar System. We're in the middle of a process of development of change existing within our current Solar System, but we know that that is not the end. We are part of the larger Galactic System. We are part of this larger Galactic process, which, I think, we want to investigate from a similar standpoint. What is a galaxy as a process of change from lower organization to higher organization, as an anti-entropic process of development, of change, something that subsumes the Solar System?

An Array of Anomalies

In some of these classes, we may get deeper into the fundamental organization of the Universe, potentially at the level of the type of shift that we went through when Einstein realized that energy and matter are a product of the same thing, $E=mc^2$, that space and time are interconnected as a single process. We went through a complete revolution in our fundamental understanding of how the Universe is organized. Some of our most basic conceptions were overturned. A lot of that relates

FIGURE 3

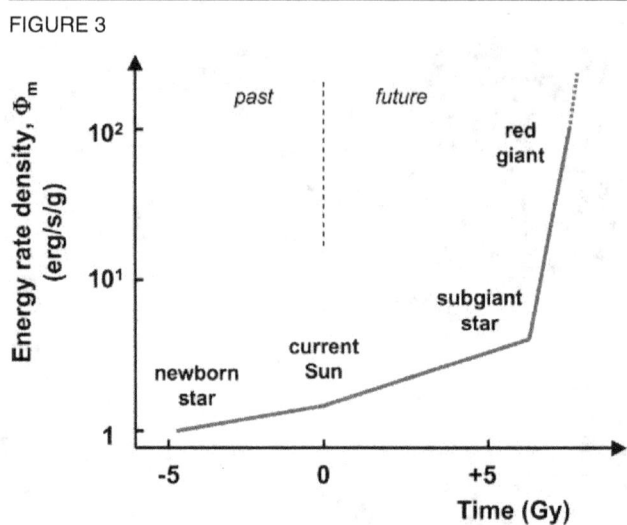

From "Energy Rate Density as a Complexity Metric and Evolutionary Driver," by E.J. Chaisson

A star's energy-flux density increases as it evolves. The figure uses our Sun as an example and shows the evolutionary sequence of such a star over billions of years (Gy) as the sequence is currently understood. Energy rate density (energy-flux density) is shown in ergs per second per gram of stellar mass.

to stellar-scale processes.

When we investigate galaxies and galactic systems, we immediately run into an array of anomalies, of problems. We can't explain some of the most basic properties of galaxies by extrapolating our current understanding of physics to this larger scale. We will take this up in more detail in the coming classes.

As a teaser, you may be familiar with all the talk about "dark matter." To some extent we can measure the rotation of galaxies—especially by looking at other galaxies, but also at our own to some degree. We can't account for how they rotate. What we observe is a mapping of the change in orbital speed of stars and other matter as you look further and further away from the center of the galaxy toward its periphery (**Figure 4**). Based on our understanding of how much mass is present in volumes at different distances from the center of a given galaxy, we would expect the mass—stars, gas, dust—to orbit at a certain speed, by using our understanding of gravitation as we understand it in our Solar System, and applying it on the galactic scale.

But what we see is that the mass orbits at a much faster speed than we can explain, especially when you move toward the outer regions. This is the basis for the hypothesis that there is something out there that we haven't been able to detect yet, but that's adding an

FIGURE 4

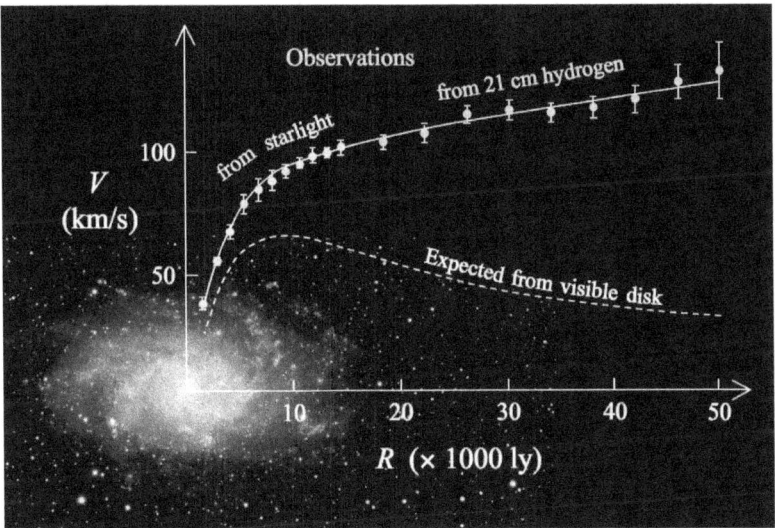

Stefania Deluca

Stars rotate around the galactic center, but not at the velocities expected from Newtonian physics. The velocities of stars are supposed to vary according to the environment: the amount of mass at the center and the distribution of mass throughout the disk. The velocity of any given star is then supposed to depend on its distance from the galactic center. Astronomers estimate the galactic mass and its distribution on the basis of the emitted light, and then calculate the rotation curve (expected velocities at different distances from the center).

In the case of the spiral galaxy M33, shown here, the result is the dashed curve. However, the actual velocities, as directly measured, are shown in the upper, solid curve. (Distance from the center is shown on the x-axis in thousands of light-years; rotational velocity is shown on the y-axis in km/second.) So what's wrong? Popular opinion among astronomers is that there must be mass that we cannot see, so-called dark matter. A halo of dark matter surrounding M33 would fix the problem. There are, of course, other possibilities.

extra gravitational effect, adding extra mass that makes it orbit at a faster rate. It's called dark matter. That's something that people are looking into. But the point is, we don't know.

We have yet to explain even how a single galaxy rotates and maintains the structure and the type of activity that it does. You have an array of fascinating properties associated with some mysterious, super-massive object at the center, which we think is at the center of basically every galaxy. We've got the best evidence in our own Galaxy, where we've been able to see stars orbiting around some point in space, in the center of our galaxy, where we see nothing; and the expectation is that this is a super-massive black hole.

What is that? It's where our equations go to infinity. It's where space-time goes to infinity. It's where basically our equations literally break down. We don't know. We know there is something going on at the center of our Galaxy that seems to be causing an effect

equivalent to a mass of four million times the mass of our Sun, causing stars to orbit on a time scale of 10 or 20 years—stars the size of our Sun, orbiting a point where we see nothing. Is it some kind of super-massive object? Whatever it is, we don't understand the physics of it.

We see relationships in galaxies between the mass of this super-massive object and properties of the galaxy as a whole, which we can't explain. The mechanisms that we know of, by which this super-massive object would interact with the galaxy as a whole, give us no explanation for how they maintain a coherent relationship, a certain coherent resonance with each other. That's another anomaly that we see.

We see some galaxies that look like this one, the galaxy called Hercules A (**Figure 5**). The galaxy itself—hundreds of billions of stars—is entirely in that bright little central region there. So at visible wavelengths, that's what you see as a galaxy. It's not a little tiny galaxy; it's a big one.

But when we look at it in other parts of the electromagnetic spectrum—in radio waves, for example—we see those massive structures of plasma—electrically charged gas—shooting out from the galaxy, that maintain coherence and structure on a scale that dwarfs the size of the galaxy itself. Astrophysicists think this phenomenon is associated with the apparently super-massive object at the center of the galaxy. There have been theories to explain how this happens, and then observational evidence overturning those theories, and then new theories.

So it's a new area of investigation. Here again we see cases of incredibly energetic activity and incredible masses at a point where our current level of physics just completely breaks down—the equations literally go to infinity.

The Solar System in the Galaxy

These are just some of the provocative, unanswered questions with respect to the structure of a galactic system as a whole. Another approach, which we've worked on, is to look at how changes on Earth have a remarkable correspondence with the passage of the Solar System through different environments as the

FIGURE 5

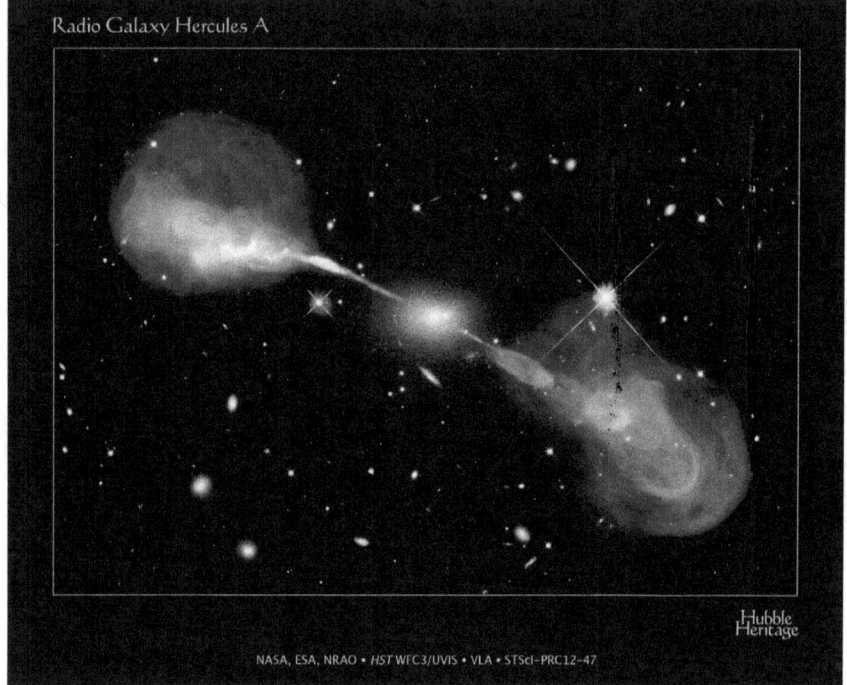

Radio Galaxy Hercules A

NASA, ESA, NRAO • *HST* WFC3/UVIS • VLA • STScI–PRC12-47

NASA, ESA, NRAO, STScI, et al.

Radio Galaxy Hercules A: Plasma jets in opposite directions are a feature of the supergiant elliptical galaxy at the center. The jets—of subatomic particles in a magnetic field (plasma)—are ejected at relativistic speeds, that is, at some appreciable fraction of the speed of light, and are visible only at non-visible wavelengths such as radio (the color is computer generated, possibly to indicate the temperature gradient). The galaxy itself is a thousand times more massive than our Home Galaxy and its central mass of 2.5 billion solar masses is a thousand times that of the central mass in our Galaxy. This composite was created by superimposing the image in radio waves, taken by the Very Large Array in New Mexico, on an image at visible wavelengths taken by the Hubble Space Telescope.

Sun and the Solar System orbit the center of the Galaxy. This is most clearly expressed in climate, where we see—in the very, very long-term records of climate on earth—a remarkable correspondence between large-scale climate change (the stuff that makes the greenies really freak out) and different environments within our Galaxy that our Solar System has experienced.

The Solar System bobs up and down, above and below the Galactic plane, as it orbits the center of the Galaxy; we see clear indications of climate changes corresponding to that cycle. The Solar System also passes into and out of the Galaxy's spiral arms. (**Figure 6**) We see very large-scale changes in the climate of our planet that correspond to the record of our passage through the spiral arm structures.

But there are also other, even more provocative correlations between geophysical activity, including large-scale volcanic activity, with some of these cycles. The Basement Team has talked extensively about the seeming resonance of the evolution of life with some of these cycles. In the fossil record, you get extinctions and mass extinctions—wipe-outs of large numbers of species—but also the generation of new species and accelerated rates of the appearance of new species called radiations. There are certain cycles of extinctions and speciations that correspond to the events in our travels through the Galaxy.

You have, therefore, an array of fascinating questions that should be looked at from the standpoint of a single investigation. What is this Galactic System that we're a part of? What are the principles governing the organization and the structure of a single galactic system? What is the physics? What about the discrepant orbital speeds of stars, and this issue of the relations between the supermassive central objects and the structure of the Galaxy as a whole? And what are the relations between processes on Earth and in our Solar System—climatological, geophysical, biological—and the different environments in our Galaxy that we've experienced?

All of this converges on one question: What is this Galaxy that we're a part of? We are not just seeking some new mathematical laws that will describe how stars orbit the galactic center. If you go online you can find a lot of people who have a lot of theories, loads of explanations. "I got this. I got that. I got it all figured out." The Internet is full of that stuff. But our key question is, how can mankind come to a higher level of understanding of the principles organizing these galactic systems? What would it mean for mankind to understand that?

Mankind in the Universe

This brings us to the point of asking, what is mankind here in the Universe? What is our "location" in the Universe? Mankind can be seen as moving through a

FIGURE 6

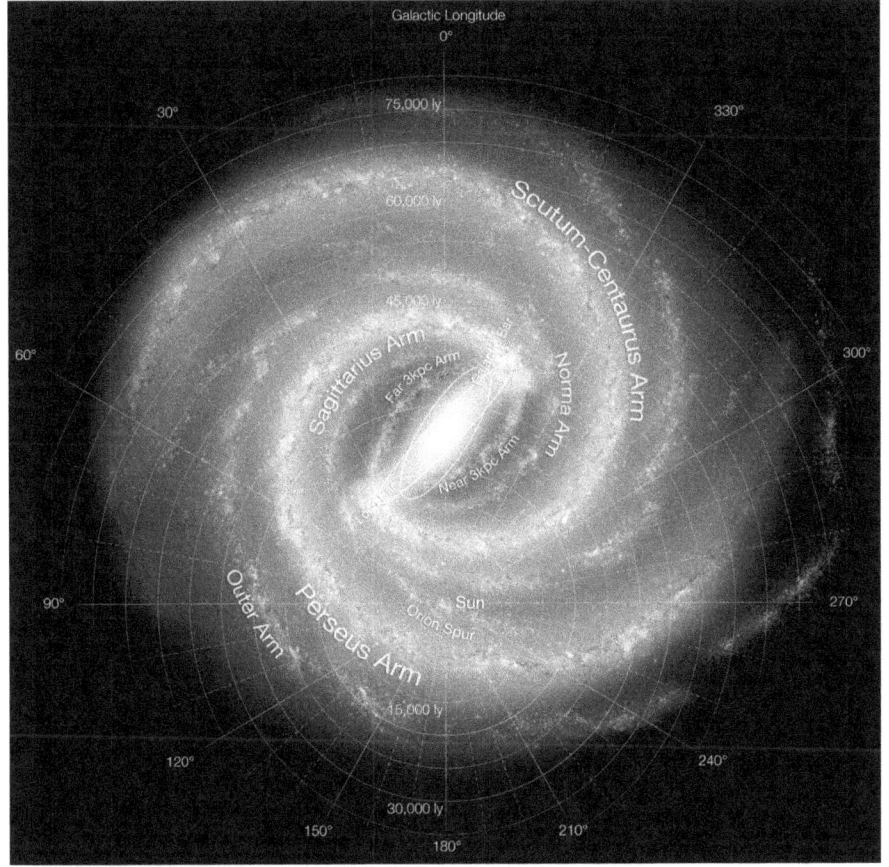

NASA/JPL-Caltech/ESO/R. Hunt

You are here: The Sun is at the point from which the galactic longitude lines radiate. This is an artist's visualization of the best data we have on the structure of our Galaxy, including visual, radiowave, and other data. (Where would your telescope have to be to obtain such an image?) Note the bar at the galactic center, making ours a barred spiral. The labels use two units of distance: the light year is the distance travelled by light in one year, about 6 trillion miles (see, for example, 75,000 ly), and the kiloparsec or kpc, about 3,260 light years or 19 thousand trillion miles (see, for example, Far 3kpc Arm).

ideas about how they are created over geological time scales—you are looking at mankind creating his means of existence based on relating to a different process. We are no longer just relating to the process of the biosphere at the given time. We are relating to it as a geological phenomenon.

But then we have the process of moving to a new stage, a new platform, where we begin to sustain ourselves, and create a new level of existence based on processes which have nothing to do with the biosphere, which are not products of the biosphere. In a nuclear stage of existence of mankind, in which it controls the processes of the nucleus—fission and fusion—we exist in a relationship to what I would call a stellar principle, relating to materials and processes that are a product of a stellar principle, of a stellar process. The array of elements of the periodic table is the gift created for us by the stars going through their life cycles and their anti-entropic processes.

To Fight for the Next Step

So what is next? We have a lot more to do, obviously, on these levels, but we have a whole new perspective of what would it mean for mankind to be an actually Galactic species. And again, to dishonor Star Wars, we're not talking about flying around to different places in the Galaxy. We are describing a sacred process of mankind generating new conceptions that enable the human species to interact with the Universe in a fundamentally different way, in a higher order relationship. You see it in the transition from mankind just existing as an organizing force in the biosphere, to mankind moving to being an organizing force in the Solar System. And it's the discoveries of the science of the Solar System at these deeper levels of physical science which enabled it, which created that, for mankind.

Our mission is to fight for the creation of the next step, to pursue these higher order questions of what is

series of platforms. Mankind's existence, development, and progress in the very early phases, was purely tied to how mankind could improve his understanding of living processes on Earth, and control and improve them to improve his own condition. So we improved our existence by mediating our relationship to the biosphere through our understanding.

We began to do some interesting things: We began to relate not just to the biosphere as it existed at the time. We began to relate to it as a geological evolutionary process. We began to use fossil fuels, for example, something that is not a product of the biosphere at any arbitrary time. We had burned wood, but wood, unlike fossil fuels, is produced continuously. When society begins to depend on something like fossil fuels—according to the mainstream governing galactic systems—what are the principles underlying them, including some of the anomalous phenomena I just breezed through, and others that we may not even know yet. And to address what it is going to mean for mankind to rise to that level.

That is a broad overview. The idea of this series is to get into a number of these topics in more detail, and in a more pedagogical fashion—define what we know, what we don't yet know, what are the questions, what are the assumptions. We will also address the methodological outlook that should really guide our work.

The Living and the Non-Living

Question: On Vernadsky, and his idea of the biochemical migration of atoms, did he think that any atom, let's say, died? Did it ever somehow disappear?

Deniston: He was definitely fascinated with radioactivity and radioactive decay. So there you get elements decaying, changing into a different element, so I think that would be the closest you'd get to an element dying, so to speak. (**Figure 7**)

What I find interesting about his approach is that he's asking "what is life?" You have the same chemical elements in living and non-living activities, the oxygen in the atmosphere: We breathe it; it comes in and out of life. The food we eat: Its chemical elements were part of non-living processes and became part of living processes. They are returned to non-living processes. So you have this exchange with this medium, this structure of the Earth's crust, with these certain chemical elements, that exist on the Earth's surface.

What I think is fascinating is, how do you define, not just what the stuff is, but what's the organizing principle? Why does it behave in a certain way, and not in another way? I'm not an expert on all of Vernadsky's work, so I'm not going to say I can completely answer how he thought about this. But from my reading of what is available in English in some of his work, I was fascinated—he seems to be looking for how to narrow down and define and forcefully demonstrate certain processes of change, or states of organization, which tell us that something different is acting to create what we call living; how to find certain states of organization of the Earth's surface, the biogeochemical medium, that you can identify as the footprint of a principle of life—and in a similar way, unique footprints for human life.

We use the same elements. We don't have special elements. But we are able to organize states of organi-

FIGURE 7

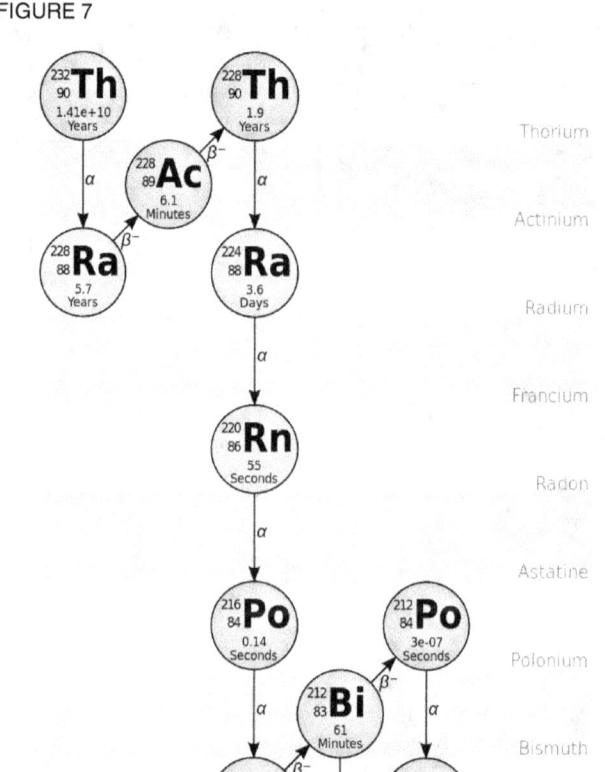

Wikimedia Commons/BatesIsBack

The thorium cascade is an example of the decay of one radioactive atom into another, and another, until a stable atom is the result. The atoms are properly called nuclides, that is, nuclear species, defined by the number of protons and neutrons in the nucleus. Thorium (Th), for example, always has 90 protons, but the number of neutrons is not always the same. Lead (Pb) always has 82 protons, but again, the number of neutrons varies.

The thorium cascade, as shown above, begins with thorium-232 (232 is the total of protons and neutrons). Thorium-232 emits an alpha particle (α), that is, a particle of two protons and two neutrons, to become radium-228, which in turn emits a negatively charged beta particle (β^-, also known as an electron) to become actinium-228. (The alpha-beta terminology was developed when the nature of these emissions was still not known.) The decay process eventually ends with the formation of lead-208, which is stable, that is, not radioactive.

zation of the biospheric system that you would never see manifested under the principle of just life, or just animal life. You can define this as the unique footprint of some other principle acting, some human creative principle expressed, not in the object, but in the state of organization and in the process.

Galactic Structure

Question: I have a question about the idea of the system of the Galaxy. I think you'll probably get into this in future classes, when you start going through these anomalies that we've run into, but can you give an idea of what we're talking about, what we mean by a *system* of a Galaxy? I'm not even sure what we're trying to define. The Solar System seems a little easier because it's fairly simple, in a sense, but the Galaxy is just—I'm not really sure what problems we're trying to solve, what questions we're trying to answer.

Deniston: We have a giant blob of stars. (Points to image of spiral galaxy underlying the rotation curves, **Figure 4**.) We see an incredible amount of structure, spiral arms, really nice structures, and beautiful, very thin discs, other components. There is a lot of structure, which is fascinating to investigate in and of itself. But then, there are some outright anomalies about how that structure behaves. In our current understanding of how gravitation works, of how bodies orbit around a mass, the orbit is determined by the distances and the amount of mass they are orbiting. Based upon those conceptions, and what we think we can estimate as the amount of mass that is present, what we see shouldn't be happening. We can't explain why it is happening.

Take a simple example of an anomaly: In a planetary system, all of the planets orbit in the same direction, and you don't expect to see a planet in retrograde motion. It would be an anomaly; it shouldn't be there, based upon your conception about what's actually happening up there.

This is a little bit more sophisticated, obviously. But our current conceptions about gravitation and mass don't seem to work for just the basic question, how do things orbit around the Galaxy? And so the leading idea is that there must be other forms of mass, of matter, out there, which we haven't found yet, and might be very, very hard to detect, so-called dark matter that's adding the extra mass effect, that is causing this deviation in how we see the Galaxy rotate.

Dark matter has not been found. Still, it's the hypothesis most people are pursuing. Some people have other hypotheses. Across the array of issues we want to cover, I think we want to look for new levels of science, new physical principles. We want to further and further refine and demonstrate that there has to be some other

principle acting, and then try to track it down, just as Kepler pursued Mars. The way he talked about it was that he thought he had it chained up, and then it broke the chains and got away.

What's the actual cause of the organization, the type of activity we see in these systems? The thesis I'm working from is that our understanding of mankind's position in the Universe is going to give us new levels of ability to interact with the Universe, yielding new domains of science and a potential for new technologies. This means a new, higher level of existence for mankind, based upon redefining our existence from the standpoint of our relationship to the principles of the Universe that are responsible for the existence, structure, development, and governing of galactic systems.

A few of the world-renowned astronomers of the past century were pursuing an idea about how galaxies are created and how they evolve which is very different from the standard, entropic view. It has not been disproven. It has just been pushed aside and disregarded.

The Armenian astronomer Viktor Ambartsumian, based on his observations, developed the theoretical framework of how galaxies are being created and ejected from the nuclei of other galaxies. He was convinced that galaxies exhibit much more of a creative, developing process than is found in the standard Big Bang cosmology, where you get one mysterious instant of creation and everything just unfolds—entropically. Some cosmologists literally say you've got a lot of gas in a really big box, and that's what the Universe is.

Ambartsumian couldn't be *entirely* ignored because he was already respected for much of his earlier work. The American, Halton Arp, was another respected astronomer who turned to the study of certain observed properties of galaxies that conflict with the accepted wisdom. His work seems to show, again, that there are levels of science we haven't yet achieved.

Are New Principles 'Allowed'?

Question: Is it acknowledged by scientists that there might be new principles involved?

Deniston: No. The general approach is to work out how to explain everything we observe from the standpoint of just what we know now.

To some degree there are the questions of dark matter, dark energy. Those are open questions. I don't have a full overview on where different people in the academic community stand on introducing new physical principles to explain some of these things. But the work of Arp and

Ambartsumian, for example,—that whole direction of investigation has been pushed aside, because in astrophysics it shouldn't be able to happen, so therefore it's not happening.

It reminds me of the situation in the Nineteenth Century, when scientists began to realize from geological evidence that the Earth has been in existence for hundreds of millions, actually a few billion years. This led to a question about what fuel the Sun is burning. If Earth has existed that long, what must the Sun be burning, such that it could continue to put out energy for that amount of time? Any conceivable energy source known at that time would have been consumed in thousands or hundreds of thousands of years. No chemical reaction or burning process could sustain the Sun for so long. Could you have said," Well then, let's just pretend we didn't find all that geological stuff, because then the problem doesn't arise?" People were thinking that the Sun might somehow get refueled.

We didn't have the ability to solve the problem at that time. We didn't have the level of science necessary to enable us to ever answer that question. It's perfectly valid and correct to approach this galactic question in a similar way. We see some super-energetic activity, and incredible structure and organization emanating from the point where our mathematical physics goes to infinity. Maybe there is something more fundamental there that we don't yet understand, that could be as revolutionary as these earlier revolutionary discoveries. That's the type of pursuit we want to reopen.

Then again, recognize that we're looking at developing systems. The whole Universe—these nested hierarchies—what we know is that we see processes moving towards higher energy-flux densities, higher states of organization. We have yet to understand the real nature of our Universe as fundamentally creative.

Spiral and Elliptical Galaxies

Question: Are all the galaxies that spiral type of . . .

Deniston: Not all of them. Just for reference, this is a giant molecular cloud within our Galaxy (**Figure 2**). It is a tiny, tiny, tiny little region of our Galaxy. You've got to imagine, this spiral Galaxy (**Figure 4**, background) has probably tens of billions of stars. It's a mind-boggling number. We're looking at something that has an incredible amount of structure and fine resolution that you can't see at this level. Relative to this spiral Galaxy image, the giant molecular cloud is

Creative Commons/Alissa Arp
American astronomer Halton Arp (1927-2013)

Armenian astronomer and astrophysicist Viktor Amazaspovich Ambartsumian (1908-1996)

zoomed-in really far. It would be like looking at me and then looking at a picture of one of my cells. It's probably an even bigger difference of scale than that.

There are generally two types of galaxies, but with a fair amount of variation. Large, highly-organized galactic structures are usually either these spiral structures, or what are called elliptical galaxies that are spheroidal. The ellipticals are like giant balls. They don't have the thin disc or the spiral arms. In a two-dimensional projection, they look like elliptical or circular discs because of their spheroidal structure.

There are all kinds of variation within each of type of galaxy. Are the spiral arms wound tightly together? Are they stretched out? Some spiral galaxies have a bar that looks just like a rigid structure, which orbits around the center. You also get a bunch of smaller, more irregular galaxies that are not as presentable—amorphous cloud or blob structures. They are probably just as fascinating. But the larger, more highly organized ones tend to either be spiral or elliptical.

Time Scales of Cosmic Effects

Question: Are you saying that the Galaxy has an effect on climate change and other phenomena? Does it cause the seasons to change? Is the Galaxy changing the leaf colors themselves, or is it because maybe the Sun's blocking—or not blocking?

Deniston: If it is, it's doing a really good job. It looks pretty nice this time of year. Climate change tends to be on really long time scales. If you're looking at something you'd call active Galactic influence on climate change, it's a continuous factor that's active at all times. The work of Henrik Svensmark, Nir Shaviv, and others shows, that the cosmic radiation effect—that's penetrating the biosphere at all times, that's coming from the larger Galactic System—plays a significant role in clouds forming. So that's a constant input. It's always there. As our Solar System moves into different parts of the Galaxy, where that input changes, then that changes how much effect we get on Earth from our Galactic input.

For example, if you take the past 500 million years, we've been through four cycles between what are called ice-house and hot-house modes of climate. **(Figure 8)** We're currently in ice-house mode. In hot-house mode, there are no ice caps on the poles at all, no ice caps top or bottom, and the climate is significantly warmer. Shaviv found that our periods of hot-house mode occurred when the Solar System was traveling between two spiral arms, and these are environments where we think we receive less of this Galactic cosmic radiation, meaning less cloud cover and more sunlight coming all the way down and reaching the Earth, not being reflected by the clouds. Because the clouds do a lot; it's like your umbrella, you don't want to get a tan like me. The umbrella can block the Sun. Clouds reflect a lot of the sunlight.

The theory that these guys are working on, is that with fewer cosmic rays, there is less contribution to cloud formation. You get fewer clouds. You get more sunlight coming down and hitting the Earth. You get a warmer climate overall. And you get the inverse effect when we're traveling through regions of the Galaxy where we have a lot of cosmic radiation coming in, causing a lot more cloud cover, which reflects sunlight much more, contributing to an overall cooler climate. So there are periods when the ice caps move much farther towards the Equator—huge ice caps covering big chunks of the Earth.

So these are massive changes, with climate going from everything being Southern California and hotter, to everything being Boston—frigid and cold. Very large-scale changes in climate tend to coincide with the passages into and out of spiral arms.

That's an example of the large-scale climate change effects. You see it over very long time-scales. Then you get smaller effects on shorter time-scales when the Sun gets more magnetically active, or less active, and that magnetic field shields Earth from some of the Galaxy's cosmic rays. So that can contribute to changes on shorter time scales such as decades or a few years.

I don't know if the Environmental Protection Agency has yet considered cosmic radiation a pollutant, or not. We're inquiring about that. (Laughter) Physicists are

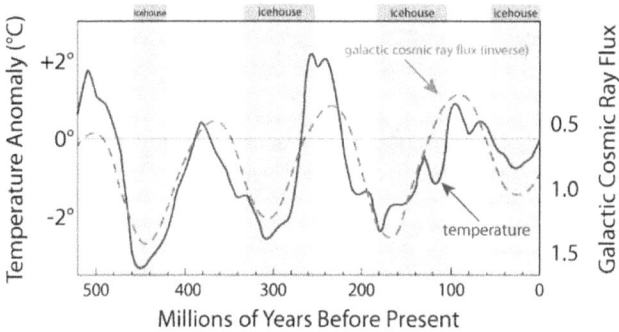

FIGURE 8

GALACTIC COSMIC RAY FLUX AND TEMPERATURE

Earth's temperature fluctuates inversely with the flow of cosmic rays from the Galaxy, as shown here. The low points correspond to what have been called Ice Ages.

worried they're going to have to shut down the Large Hadron Collider for emitting pollutants.

CO_2 Not a Climate Changer

The study of 500-million-year hot-house and ice-house modes was famous, because over that time, the Earth's climate went through four of the big changes from hot-house—no ice caps at all, much higher sea level—down to ice-house—a lot colder, big ice caps. It went back and forth four times, and the CO_2 level only changed twice. This was shown about 20 years ago, that on these longer time scales, CO_2 does not look like a major contributor to climate change at all. It's just doing its own thing. The climate's doing one thing. The CO_2 is doing something else. That upset a lot of people, because CO_2 is supposed to be the *only* thing that causes change, according to the current propaganda paradigm.

It was Jan Veizer in Canada who showed that, and then Nir Shaviv, the American-Israeli researcher, found that study, and then said, "Oh, look, not only is CO_2 not correlated with climate change, but the climate change in these records is closely correlated with the spiral arm travels of our Solar System." And that was one of the key studies that went into launching the investigation of galactic effects on climate change.

Meanwhile the plants are screaming for more CO_2.

So, that may be good for tonight. It's getting a little bit late. I would like to take up various elements of this presentation in a little more detail and in a more pedagogical way, to sink our teeth into how we know some of these things. What do we know about how our Solar System is trucking through the Galaxy? What do we know about these properties?

Every Day Counts In Today's Showdown To Save Civilization

That's why you need EIR's **Daily Alert Service**, a strategic overview compiled with the input of Lyndon LaRouche, and delivered to your email 5 days a week.

For example: On November 5, EIR's Daily Alert featured Lyndon LaRouche's warning that Obama can and must be removed immediately, to avoid Obama's push for thermonuclear confrontation with Russia. That issue identified The Drone Papers put out by Glenn Greenwald's The Intercept as the Pentagon Papers of 2015—damning Barack Obama as a mass murderer, and providing the evidence for his Constitutional removal from office.

That edition also featured EIR's exclusive report on a hearing called by Rep. John Conyers on Capitol Hill to expose the dangers represented by Obama's actions—a hearing all but suppressed by other media.

This is intelligence you need to act on, if we are going to survive as a nation and a species. Can you really afford to be without it?

THURSDAY, NOVEMBER 5, 2015

EIR Daily Alert Service

EIR DAILY ALERT SERVICE P.O. BOX 17390, WASHINGTON, DC 20041-0390

- Dump Obama Now or Face Thermonuclear Holocaust
- Extraordinary Capitol Hill Event Warns of Obama Thermonuclear War Provocations against Russia
- Rep. Tulsi Gabbard: Unlawful for U.S. To Wage War in Syria
- Satanic Environmentalist Offensive Launched in U.S.
- O'Malley Campaign Support Grows in Iowa, Key Democrats Say
- Behind the New York Times Headlines on 'Death in Middle Age'
- QE Inflated Wall Street, Screwed Main Street—Says Wall Street
- Russian Defense Ministry Coordinating with Syrian Opposition against ISIS
- Frontex: Arrest Illegal Immigrants!
- Bavaria Considering a Constitutional Case against Merkel
- U.S.-Russian Communications Test over Syria
- Malaysia and ASEAN Stand Up To Obama's Threats over South China Sea
- Barenboim's Orchestra Plays Mozart for Peace in the Middle East

EDITORIAL

Dump Obama Now or Face Thermonuclear Holocaust

✂